Beyond Self-Esteem

G000092396

Developing a Genuine Sense of Human Value

RESEARCH MONOGRAPH OF THE NATIONAL ASSOCIATION
FOR THE EDUCATION OF YOUNG CHILDREN, VOLUME 4

Beyond Self-Esteem: Developing a Genuine Sense of Human Value

**Nancy E. Curry and
Carl N. Johnson**

National Association for the Education of Young Children
Washington, DC

To J.T. McL., who has enhanced my self-understanding and self-esteem through his support, challenges, and most of all, his acceptance. (NEC)

To my parents, who provided my first awareness of the dynamic balance between acceptance and the need to achieve. (CNJ)

Photo credits: Hildegard Adler, *p. 22, 59;* Nancy P. Alexander, *p. 29, 103;* Subjects & Predicates, *p. 33, 36, 70, 134;* Ginger Howard, *p. 43;* Francis Wardle, *p. 47;* © Jim Bradshaw 1990, *p. 51, 106;* © Crystal Images 1990, *p. 57;* Beth Chepote, *p. 77;* Barbara Brockmann, *p. 81;* public domain, *p. 85, 125;* Elisabeth Nichols, *p. 100, 122;* © Renee Stockdale 1990, *p. 116;* © Cheryl Namkung, *p. 139;* Skjold Photographs, *p. 144;* Kay Freeman, *p. 158;* Dianne Carter, *p. 160.*

National Association for the Education of Young Children
1834 Connecticut Avenue, N.W.
Washington, DC 20009–5786

The National Association for the Education of Young Children attempts through its publications program to provide a forum for discussion of major issues and ideas in our field. We hope to provoke thought and promote professional growth. The views expressed or implied are not necessarily those of the Association.

Library of Congress Catalog Card Number: 90-62662

ISBN 0–935989–39–0

NAEYC #143

Book production: Jack Zibulsky

PRINTED IN THE UNITED STATES OF AMERICA.

About the Authors

Nancy E. Curry is Professor in the Child Development and Child Care Program in the School of Social Work, and holds joint appointments with the Schools of Health Related Professions, Medicine, and Education at The University of Pittsburgh. She has written numerous articles on sociodramatic play as a curricular and therapeutic tool. Her special interests include affective and social development of young children and quality child care.

Carl N. Johnson is an Associate Professor in the Child Development and Child Care Program in the School of Social Work, University of Pittsburgh. Teaching in an applied program with a continuing interest in basic research, he has long struggled to make bridges between research and practice, hard science and clinical intuition. He is currently studying young children's concepts of magic and early self-understanding.

v

Source Notes

Page 21. Reprinted with permission of International Universities Press From "Ego and reality in psychoanalytic theory" by R.W. White in *Psychological Issues, Monograph 3.* Copyright © 1963 by International Universities Press.

Page 31. Reprinted with permission of Merrill, an imprint of Macmillan Publishing Company from *Teaching Infants and Preschoolers with Handicaps* by Donald B. Bailey, Jr., and Mark Wolery. Copyright © 1984.

Pages 48–49. Reprinted with permission of Erlbaum Publishers from "A developmental theory of friendship and acquaintanceship processes" by J. Gottman and J. Parkhurst in W. Collins (Ed.), *Minnesota symposium on child psychology, vol. 13.* Copyright © 1980.

Page 50. From *Children's Friendships* by Z. Rubin. Reprinted with permission of Harvard University Press. Copyright © 1980 by Harvard University Press. All rights reserved.

Page 53. From *Bad Guys Don't Have Birthdays: Fantasy Play at 4* by Vivian G. Paley. Reprinted by permission of The University of Chicago Press. Copyright © 1988 by The University of Chicago Press. All rights reserved.

Page 73. Shepard, L.A. and M.E. Smith. Synthesis of research on school readiness and kindergarten retention. *Educational Leadership 44,* pp. 78–86. Reprinted with permission of the Association for Supervision and Curriculum Development. Copyright © 1986 by the Association for Supervision and Curriculum Development. All rights reserved.

Pages 94–95. From *The Magic Years* by Selma H. Fraiberg. Copyright © 1959 Selma H. Fraiberg; copyright renewed. Reprinted with permission of Charles Scribner's Sons, an imprint of the Macmillan Publishing Company.

Page 110. From *Beginnings of Social Understanding* by J. Dunn. Reprinted with permission of Basil Blackwell, Inc. Copyright © 1988 by Basil Blackwell, Inc. All rights reserved.

Page 119. From *Bad Guys Don't Have Birthdays: Fantasy Play at 4* by Vivian G. Paley. Reprinted by permission of The University of Chicago Press. Copyright © 1988 by The University of Chicago Press. All rights reserved.

Acknowledgments

THE AUTHORS WOULD LIKE TO ACKNOWLEDGE the editorial help of Janet Brown McCracken. Her suggestions, recastings of material, and steady hand facilitated progress of this endeavor and greatly enhanced the final product. Polly Greenberg's dream in creating this volume may have seemed nightmarish at times, but her conviction, suggestions, exhortations, assurance, and decision to bring Jan into the project brought it to fruition.

To Colleen Scholl we extend our appreciation for her willingness to do the word processing of innumerable editions of the manuscript, often done above and beyond her regular departmental duties. The additional secretarial help of Virginia Rhodes and Mary Pat Campbell in the School of Social Work furthered our work. Grace Gibbons-Brown's help in checking references was invaluable. To our colleague Ursula Schwartz we extend thanks for her thoughtful and informed review of the manuscript; her suggestions have strengthened the book immensely. The staff of the Carnegie Mellon and University of Pittsburgh Child Care Centers were also very helpful in sharing their professional insights and experiences, grounding self-esteem in model practices.

The labors of Catherine Martin (age 10), Sarah Martin (age 8), and Kristy Scholl (age 9), in copying, collating, and numbering material during the press of one deadline, were truly lifesavers for this project and the authors.

Contents

Preface

FROM INFANCY, WE STRIVE TO MAINTAIN a sense of significance, purpose, and value in our lives. Poets, philosophers, psychologists, and theologians alike have recognized this fundamental human aspiration. Professionals in early childhood education, too, have long accepted our prime responsibility to promote children's inner sense of significance and value. Unlike more objective educational or therapeutic goals, concern about self-esteem turns attention to children's own sense of significance and value. Hence, the goal is not merely to get children to read or act better, but to get them to experience themselves as valuable and competent individuals.

The strength of the idea of self-esteem, however, is rivaled only by its weakness. True, the concept touches the essence of the human spirit. But it is also open to serious misconception and trivialization. Happy-grams, empty praise, smiley-face stickers, "participant" ribbons, and all manner of drivel are lavished upon children under the guise of building their self-esteem. In a culture plagued by self-preoccupation and narcissism, it is hard to know whether pleas for improved self-esteem are a solution or part of the problem.

Most disturbing, perhaps, is the idea that self-esteem is a cure-all. One preschool child was referred to a clinic for language delay, acting out, unsupportive parents, and poor peer relations. The clinicians' treatment plan: Improve the child's low self-esteem. Are we to suppose that this child's sense of self could be transformed without dealing with the complex and depressing realities of his life? All too many interventions aimed at improving self-esteem have been similarly vague and ineffective (Strein, 1988).

Low self-esteem can be viewed as the root of all sorts of social ills — alcoholism, drug abuse, crime, teenage pregnancy, school failure, and unemployment. The state of California even has established a commission on self-esteem in order to alleviate society's ills. While concluding that "self-esteem is the likeliest candidate for a social vaccine" (California Task Force, 1990, p. 4), its comprehensive analysis shows that there is no single, simple cure. To begin with, they found it essential to distinguish *self-esteem* from *highly individualistic narcissism* by defining it to include not only a sense of self-worth and importance, but also "the character to be accountable for myself and to act responsibly toward others" (p. 1). This definition points to the breadth and complexity of the problem. Beyond esteem in the narrow sense, we are talking about the development of character, values, self-control, and morality! (You think a cure for cancer is difficult?)

Using a broader framework for understanding self-esteem, this monograph pulls together a knowledge base of recent child development research and practice. Going beyond traditional, global measures of self-esteem, new measures offer a more differentiated and integrated picture of self-development. For the first time, objective science is proving the importance and early development of the subjective self, thereby enhancing long-held beliefs of early childhood professionals. These findings are confidence-building! But we also must caution about the need for humility. Self-development is a complex phenomenon that should not be treated lightly. Far be it that we think we have all the answers. Yet, we can chart some clear directions: Guides for teachers, administrators, and professors who are seeking to better understand and promote self-development.

Part I

Beyond self-esteem: How young children develop a sense of value

Introduction

What is self-esteem?

SELF-ESTEEM IS NOT A WELL-DEFINED CONCEPT. It is, rather, an intuitive notion that has stimulated and variously guided research and practice. As Harter (1983) explains, "In most treatments of the topic, self-esteem is never clearly defined, but merely taken as a given. Presumably, there is some common referent of which we are all intuitively aware" (p. 320). This is not to say that our intuitions are incorrect. They have often served us well, just as they have sometimes led us astray. The task is not to dismiss these intuitions, but to clarify and build upon them.

Intuitions and beyond

Intuitions

The concept of self-esteem includes three basic intuitions:

1. How people think and feel about themselves is important.
2. Positive self-concepts and feelings provide the confidence, energy, and optimism to master life's tasks.
3. Self-esteem is promoted by positive self-experiences.

As Rutter (1987) points out, each of these intuitions has proved to be on the right track:

1. A growing body of literature attests to the importance of people's concepts and feelings about themselves.
2. The available evidence suggests that it is protective to have a well-established feeling of one's own worth as a person together with a confidence and conviction that one can cope with life's challenges.
3. The limited evidence suggests that two types of experiences are most influential: secure and harmonious love relationships, and successful accomplishment of tasks important to the individual. (p. 327)

Beyond intuition

Although sending us in the right direction, the concept of self-esteem suffers in being so general. All the many concepts and thoughts people have about themselves are boiled down to a single positive or negative characterization. Hence, too often self-esteem comes to be viewed as a single, fixed entity, rather than a many-sided, dynamic process.

This monograph goes beyond this single-entity notion of self-esteem in several respects.

Beyond global conceptions. Self-esteem is a cover term for many different concepts and feelings about the self. We can conceive of many different parts of ourselves: our bodies, minds, social standing, even our clothes and ancestors which we identify as ours (James, 1890). In turn, our feelings, positive or negative, about these different parts may be of very different kinds. We may feel positive about ourselves in being confident and proud, loved and accepted, powerful and controlled, or good and helpful.

Theorists have commonly distinguished four different dimensions of self-esteem: *acceptance, power and control, moral worth,* and *competence.* Instead of summarizing across these different dimensions, as was done with traditional measures of self-esteem, it is important to consider how different aspects of self-feeling may be separate or related (see Harter, 1983).

Beyond dichotomy. Self-esteem is often treated as if it is either positive or negative, good or bad. Positive self-esteem is associated with all the good things in life, whereas negative self-esteem is associated with all the bad. Hence, children with positive self-esteem are assumed to be confident, achieving, autonomous, and friendly; whereas children with low self-esteem are presumed to be unsure, incompetent, dependent, and retiring. These are stereotypes. In reality most children and adults fall somewhere in between these polarities. We all have islands of personal strength and vulnerability.

Dichotomous thinking is also evident in the idea that good feelings about the self are always healthy, whereas bad self-feelings are to be avoided. But good feelings about the self can be self-deceptive and narcissistic (excessive pride) just as bad feelings can be constructive and energizing (healthy guilt). Moreover, the most adaptive self-concepts probably arrive from coping experiences in which negative states are transformed into positive ones (Rutter, 1987; Tronick, 1989). Beyond trying to get children to "feel good" about themselves, it is important to consider how children develop an honest, adaptable, balanced sense of self.

Beyond an isolated entity. It is misleading to think of self-esteem as an isolated thing that you get. This is the inoculation theory, as if self-esteem is like a drug that can be given in a single booster shot. Instead, self-esteem must be viewed as a life-long developmental process. How children feel and think about themselves is integrally tied to their physical, social, moral, emotional, cognitive, and personality development.

The new wave of research and practice

Self-esteem is back in. The last time it was in was in the 1950s and 60s with the parents of the *Me* generation and movements toward open schooling and affective education. It went out with back to basics and the materialistic narcissism of the 70s and 80s. But now, in the 90s, self-esteem has again come center stage. In fact, during the time this monograph was being prepared, two major scholarly books were published on the subject (Mecca, Smelser, & Vasconellos, 1989; Sternberg & Kolligan, 1990), and we have seen a sudden surge of interest in developing programs to promote self-esteem. This new wave of interest seems promising. Its success, however, will require that we learn from the pitfalls of the past.

Erikson (1950) got things off to a good start in the 50s. Based on clinical insight and brilliant intuitions, Erikson considered self-esteem as a dynamic motivational component of the ego, developing within a psychosocial context. Each phase of his developmental model marked a new interrelated dimension of self-evaluation. *Basic trust* has to do with feelings of *acceptance, autonomy* with feelings of *power, initiative and guilt* with feelings of *moral worth,* and *industry* with feelings of *competence.*

Unfortunately, the subtleties of psychodynamic thinking about self-esteem were lost both to the general public and to the science of the day. The concept was seized upon and quickly became dominant, to the exclusion of other equally important qualities of the self, such as character, self-control, and self-understanding. Slogans such as "I like you just the way you are" and "Criticize the behavior not the child" became common sense to a generation of parents who sought to protect their children from the anxieties of social responsibility, while propelling them into material and social pleasures (not a surprising reaction given the overwhelming anxieties and social changes surrounding World War II).

Lacking sophisticated theories and precise measures, scientists developed measures of global self-esteem, such as the Coopersmith and Piers-Harris inventories (Wylie, 1979). Spawning hundreds of studies, these efforts further contributed to the naive idea that self-esteem is a single isolatable entity (Harter, 1983). Moreover, the measures proved to be too abstract to be of use with young children, leaving the origins and early development of self-esteem explored only retrospectively.

Programmatic efforts to enhance self-esteem suffered from a similar fate. Although some programs were decent, many were misguided and all were inadequately evaluated. Overall, lacking clearly articulated theories, practices, and assessments, these efforts proved to be disappointing (Strein, 1988; Scheirer & Kraut, 1979).

By the 1980s it was clear that research, theory, and practice needed to go beyond self-esteem as it had previously been considered. As Rosenberg (1979) lamented, "we will never understand self-esteem unless we go beyond self-esteem" (p. 288).

The last decade has seen a tremendous change in the breadth and quality of research on the self, in part spearheaded by Harter's (1983) challenge to consider self-esteem within the broader self-system. Most of this research has gone beyond self-esteem to measure various related notions such as self-regulation, self-effectance, self-schemas, and internal working models.

Although it shares many of Erikson's original assumptions, it is encouraging that the current wave of interest in self-esteem can be built on a broader and more secure foundation of research. This foundation is buttressed by the following general advances in the field of child development.

- **New measures.** Such measures have enabled researchers for the first time to examine the very beginnings of a sense of self in infancy, as well as the self-concepts of young children. These measures provide a welcome window on children's private world of thoughts and emotions.

- **New perspectives.** Combined with new measures, research in child development has led to major changes in how we view children and their development. One particularly important theme is that children are active participants in their own development. Although this theme is familiar to most professionals, it is particularly important to apply it in the study of self-esteem.

Children are active participants in the development of their sense of self. How children view their *selves* is not simply a mirror of how others view them. Infants come into the world with their own individual characteristics. The self that is experienced will depend upon how these characteristics transact with those of the caregiving environment.

Campbell (1990) details how Jamie, an active infant who cried a lot and was difficult to soothe, grew into a wild, aggressive 3-year-old who was expelled from preschool. Jamie's temperament was already placing him at risk for feeling uncontrollable, bad, and rejected, which only fueled subsequent ongoing behavioral problems. Difficult or anxious children generally find it harder to become engaged in positive self-experiences.

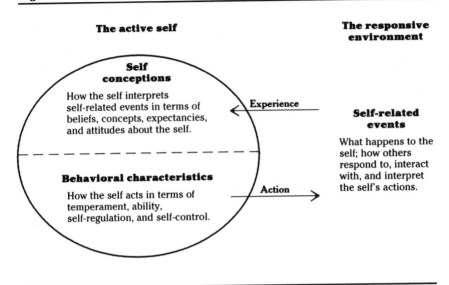

Figure 1. Interactions between self and environment.

The active self

The responsive environment

Self conceptions

How the self interprets self-related events in terms of beliefs, concepts, expectancies, and attitudes about the self.

Experience

Self-related events

What happens to the self; how others respond to, interact with, and interpret the self's actions.

Behavioral characteristics

How the self acts in terms of temperament, ability, self-regulation, and self-control.

Action

Children are not only active behaviorally, but also cognitively. Children have their own ways of viewing themselves. For example, young children's self-evaluations are often extreme and unrealistic. They may assume that by some minor infraction they caused a death or divorce, or hold grandiose ideas about their potential powers and abilities. As children get older, they get much more realistic in their self-evaluations (Stipek & Mac Iver, 1989).

These two components of children—their actual self and their concepts of this self—are completely intertwined in children's developing personalities (Eder & Mangelsdorf, in press). The child's actual self—including physical, psychological, emotional, temperamental, and social characteristics—influences her behavior and how others respond to her, which in turn influences how the child conceives of herself. Self-conceptions in turn combine with other self characteristics to influence future behavior, and so it continues (see Figure 1).

Any evaluation or intervention regarding self-esteem requires that both the actual self and the perceived self be taken into account. For example, a child with low self-esteem might be suffering with serious behavioral problems that interfere with positive self-experiences. In this case, the primary task is surely to build real skills, not to artificially boost self-esteem. In fact, the child's low self-esteem could be very functional as an honest and healthy motivator for change. In other cases, however, self-conceptions may be out of line with reality and/or dysfunctional. Misconceptions such as children's guilt about their parents' divorce, or overgeneralizations about their own bad qualities, are examples.

In practice, each child's self-understanding develops in collaboration with others. What, after all, is a child's real self? As adults, we have our views of the child's real self; the child, too, has views. Sometimes the child knows better than we do; other times we know better than the child. The goal, however, is to collaborate with the child in the development of a self that is both valued and true.

Values

Of course, this monograph is not just about research. It is equally about values. Self-esteem is fundamentally a matter of how individuals value themselves and others. We espouse values that we believe are most suited for raising children in a modern, democratic, pluralistic, post-industrial society. To this end, we espouse the universal importance of

- promoting responsive, caring, cooperative, empathetic human relationships
- providing opportunities and support for individual self-development, including the development of universally valued skills (basic education) as well as individual talents and interests
- respecting, celebrating, and learning from cultural, ethnic, and individual diversity

We also believe that tremendous resources are needed — social, psychological, spiritual, and material — to ensure that children develop the skills and character needed to function constructively in the modern world. Self-esteem is a modern problem (Cushman, 1990). In simpler times, it was relatively easy to raise children to fill a limited set of traditional cultural roles with a narrow range of skills and values. It is much harder for us all, children and adults alike, to construct and maintain valued identities in the complex, changing, pluralistic world in which we live. If nothing else, the topic of self-esteem focuses needed attention on this difficult, universal, modern problem.

How does self-esteem develop?

It should already be clear that understanding ourselves is a **lifelong** process. Self-esteem is shaped and reshaped as we interact with each other and our environment. All of us — from infants through the elderly —

are active participants in the development of our own self-esteem and that of others whose lives we touch.

When the research, clinical insights, and theories about human development are dissected and then blended, we begin to see a clearer picture of how self-esteem develops. From infancy through adulthood, the critical components of self-esteem ebb and wane, again and again, forming the threads of our human fabric (Mahler, Pine, & Bergman, 1975; Spitz, 1965; Stern, 1985).

The issues of **acceptance, power and control, moral virtue,** and **competence** (Harter, 1983) are lifelong issues, but have their roots in the early years. Infants and toddlers are developing and consolidating an initial sense of self. Preschoolers are further expanding, testing, and evaluating this self. School-age children are measuring the self against new standards.

During these years, one issue may briefly assume greater salience (e.g., power and control in toddlerhood, competence in school-age children), but all are of great importance throughout development.

Chapter 1

Infants and toddlers: Developing and consolidating a sense of self

THE DEVELOPMENT OF A SENSE OF SELF BEGINS IN INFANCY in the context of human relationships. Thus we begin this book on self-esteem by describing how infants and toddlers develop and consolidate an initial sense of self.

Infancy was once viewed as a state of "booming, buzzing confusion" (James, 1890) in which infants very gradually come to differentiate themselves from others (Mahler, Pine, & Bergman, 1975). More recent research reveals that from birth infants begin to actively organize experience in an effort to make sense of the world as it relates to them (Stern, 1985).

In either scenario — self emerging from union with another, or self as an organizer — the evidence points toward the bedrock of self-esteem: a partnership between the child and one or more loving adults. Self-esteem is the product of transactions between the active self and the responsive environment. It is a web between generations. We shall review how the process of understanding and valuing self unfolds in Part I, and then in Part II elaborate upon implications of the research and theory for caregiving.

Pregnancy

Parents' reactions to pregnancy range from elation to distress. Through those first 9 months, events are already beginning to shape the partnership between child and adults. During pregnancy, mothers tend to confirm their femininity, begin to fantasize about the child within, and perhaps intensify identifications with their own mother. Fathers may have conscious and unconscious fantasies, too, about their own masculinity being affirmed, continuity between generations, relationships with

11

parents, potential rivalry for affection, or identification with the child-to-be (Jessner, Weigert, & Foy, 1970).

Mothers may anticipate their child as a companion, burden, playmate, possession, beloved or hated sibling. These fantasies may intensify if the mother is single. Depending on the relationship with the child's father, the child may represent unity, rescue, love, a rival, an intruder, or possibly a destroyer of their relationship (Brazelton & Cramer, 1990; Jessner et al., 1970; Murphy, Mintzer, & Lipsett, 1989).

Parent expectations and feelings are already beginning to shape their response to their child, as they prepare the nursery, select names, or even attempt to deny the pregnancy (Freud, 1989b). These attitudes are the early roots of the critical partnership between adult and child, the child's sense of feeling lovable and powerful, and therefore the child's assessment of self.

Birth

Arrival of the baby is quite a shock, even for those who are fully prepared and eager for the event. Fantasies of the ideal infant are replaced with the real child (Brazelton & Cramer, 1990). A hoped-for girl may be yet another boy. The anticipated round-faced cherub may be a wrinkly squawker.

Parents sometimes report that they changed the child's name in the delivery room. "He just didn't look like an Eric." "In the delivery room, we knew she was Molly." They may be startled by their newborn's penetrating gaze (Bowlby, 1969; Klaus & Kennell, 1976). "He seemed to know us right away." Even the baby's temperament or physical characteristics may be sources of comment. "Isn't he a sweet pea?" "She's built like a gymnast."

If a baby is born with any medical condition or disability, the parents may first have to mourn the loss of the fantasied child before they can get on with the task of parenting the real baby (Drotar, Baskiewicz, Irvin, Kennell, & Klaus, 1975; Freud, A., 1965; Mintzer, Als, Tronick, & Brazelton, 1984; Murphy, Mintzer, & Lipsett, 1989; Solnit & Stark, 1961). Brazelton (1989) acknowledges the difficulty these parents face. He concludes:

> In addition to the physiological and neurological problems at-risk newborns have to cope with, they generate, by their distorted behavior, deficient parenting patterns which in turn exacerbate an already compromised start on life. (p. 419)

His concern is supported by evidence such as this:

- Brain-injured babies who appear normal can provoke responses of anger and rejection from their parents, even before the official diagnosis (Prechtl & Beintema, 1984).

- A high incidence of physical abuse is reported for children who were premature (Klein & Stern, 1971).
- A cyclical, negative interaction process often develops between parents and at-risk newborns (Als, Tronick, Adamson, & Brazelton, 1976).

Of course, many parents of at-risk children quickly learn to read their babies and respond in appropriate ways to facilitate their children's development. Professional support may be crucial to parents whose expectations of their offspring have been shattered by reality.

First-time parents, regardless of the status of their infants, find themselves challenged and at times overwhelmed with the demands of their newborn. Even before the new family leaves the hospital, then, events and personalities have begun to shape the child's self-esteem as expressed through love.

Infancy

Babies bring with them reflexes, temperament and other constitutional givens, and a readiness to relate to other human beings. They are confronted with two tasks, both of which are imbedded in issues of attachment and affective development:

1. **Regulate themselves with others.** Babies begin to establish "islands of consistency" as adults soothe, hold, feed, and otherwise nurture them.
2. **Interact with others.** Playful encounters first occur around caregiving functions (diapering, dressing, playing "This Little Piggy") and later through play with toys (Brazelton & Als, 1979). Patterns of self-control and relationships begin to form with those first diaper changes and middle-of-the-night feedings.

As infants grow, researchers and parents alike have noticed that infants seem to make developmental shifts or even quantum leaps in their development between 2 to 3 months, 5 to 6 months, 9 to 12 months, and 15 to 18 months (Stern, 1989). Note that there are overlaps in terms of timing of these stages by various theorists. These ages are ushered in with new physical or cognitive accomplishments (see Table 1). Overarching all these changes, however, are the issues of attachment and individuation of self as exhibited through affective development and self-regulation.

Birth to 3 months

Infants begin life as active participants. In fact, they possess built-in regulating capacities that we can observe as they change states from

Table 1. Developmental accomplishments in the first 3 years.

Months	Mahler	Sander	Greenspan and Greenspan	Stern	Attachment Theory Bowlby/Ainsworth	Erikson	Other Milestones
1	**Normal Autism** (0–2 months) Child has inborn regulatory capacities with a built-in stimulus barrier that lowers as parents meet needs predictably.	**I. Initial Regulation** (1–3 months) Parent helps establish regulation of the infant's basic functions through caretaking procedures. Reciprocal effects of infant on mother and mother on infant begin.	**I. Self Regulation and Interest in the World** (0–3 months)	**Emergent Self** (0–2 months) Child has inborn self-regulatory capacities to regulate interaction with others.	**Preattachment** (0–3 months)	**Trust vs. Mistrust** (oral stage) Through the experience of predictable caregiving, the child develops a sense of trustworthiness of self and others, the basis for the infant's earliest sense of identity.	**Piaget** Sensorimotor Period
2	**Symbiosis** (2–4 months) Infant experiences self and mother as dual unity; a mutual need-fulfilling system. Through predictable care, child increasingly invests in external world.		**II. Falling in Love** (2–7 months)	**Core Self** (2–6 months) Infants have a sense that they and mother are quite separate physically, are different agents, have distinctive affective experiences, and have separate histories. Various experiences that contribute to sense of core self are: 1. Self agency 2. Self coherence 3. Self affectivity 4. Self history (memory)			**Spitz** First ego organizer. Specific meaningful smile to primary caregiver(s).
3	Physiological motor and state regulation (Brazelton & Als, 1979). Orientation. Play dialogue. Beginning of object play.				**Attachment in the Making** (3–6 months)		

I. Differentiation
(4–9 months)

"Pleasure in being the cause." Intentionality and directedness in environmental exploration. Manual, tactile, and visual exploration of mother's body, one's own body, and toys. Passive Peek-A-Boo. Pushing away from mother's body. Sliding off mother's lap. Play at mother's feet. Comparative scanning of other-than-mother ("Custom's Inspection").

II. Reciprocal Exchange
(4–6 months)

Reciprocity continuing with infant becoming more active, better organized, and capable of coordinating actions with caregiver's.

III. Developing Intentional Communication
(3–10 months)

III. Initiative
(7–9 months)

Infant initiates activities to maintain social exchange with caregiver and to select and manipulate environmental encounters.

Subjective Self
(7–15 months)

Intersubjective relatedness
1. Sharing the focus of attention
2. Sharing intentions
3. Sharing affective states

Affect attunement between child and primary caregivers(s).

Phase of Clear-Cut Attachment
(6 months–3 years)

Primary Transitional Objects
(6–12 months)

Table 1. Developmental accomplishments in the first 3 years (continued).

Months	Mahler	Sander	Greenspan and Greenspan	Stern	Attachment Theory Bowlby/ Ainsworth	Erikson	Other Milestones
8							**Spitz** Second ego organizer. Stranger anxiety.
9	II. <u>Practicing</u> (9–18 months) Transitional objects. Elated investment in locomotion. "Love affair with the world." Establishing familiarity with wider world ("into everything"). Mother used for "emotional refueling" as home base after play. Active Peek-A-Boo. Beginning imitative play. Intense practice of body functions (e.g., running and being scooped up).		IV. <u>Emergence of an Organized Sense of Self</u> (9–18 months)				
10		IV. <u>Focalization</u> (10–13 months) Active manipulation of and concentration on caregiver to determine extent of her availability to meet the child's needs,					

Spitz
Third ego organizer.
Mastery of the "No."
Secondary Transitional Object
(12–24 months)

Autonomy vs. Shame and Doubt
(Anal Stage)
Holding on and letting go; alternate expressions of love and hate; needs firm and loving protection from own "potential anarchy."

Verbal Self
(15 months +)
Verbal relatedness. New way of being with primary caregiver involves:
1. Objective view of self.
2. Capacity for symbolic play.
3. Acquisition of language (which in a sense alienates child from more subjective self-experiences and togetherness of earlier periods.)

V. **Self-Assertion**
(14–20 months)
Child's new capacity to organize the world actively, to assert self, and determine own behavior, often in face of parental opposition.

III. **Rapprochment**
(15–24 months)
"Watch me"—
"Look at me"
Disappearance-reappearance play. Imitation-identification play. Play—nurturing dolls and soft toys—as well as beginning symbolic play. Social interaction—ball play. Temper tantrums. Clinging and pushing away. Mother sometimes used as extension of self. Stranger anxiety. Mastery play—toys and materials. Collect/gather; empty/fill.

Table 1. Developmental accomplishments in the first 3 years (continued).

Months	Mahler	Sander	Greenspan and Greenspan	Stern	Attachment Theory Bowlby/ Ainsworth	Erikson	Other Milestones
16 / 18		VI. Recognition (18–36 months) Capacity via language and other expressive channels to describe one's own states, intentions, and thought content.	IV. Creating Emotional Ideas (18–36 months)				Piaget Preoperational Thought
20		VII. Continuity (18–36 months) Child learns that although there are deliberate disruptions in the relationships between self and others, the self-representation and that of others remain constant.					
22 / 24	V. Consolidation of Individuality and Beginning of Emotional Object Constancy (24–36 months) Gradual achievement of self and other. Constancy in						

tion of perception of good and bad self and good and bad others. Purposeful constructive play. Beginning of fantasy, role play, and pretend.

26
28
30

VI. Emotional Thinking (30–48 months)

Emotional (libidinal) Object Constancy

Consolidation of self-representation and the representation of others. Evidence in roles children choose to play. Child can tolerate absence of parents in light of having a consistent, internalized image.

32
34
36

deep sleep, light sleep, drowsy, quiet alert, and active alert, to crying (Wolff, 1966). Experts have labeled this period:

- *Preattachment* (Bowlby, 1969)
- *Normal autism and beginning symbiosis* (Mahler, Pine, & Bergman, 1975)
- *Initial regulation* (Sander, 1975)
- *Self-regulation and interest in the world* (Greenspan & Greenspan, 1985)
- *Emerging self* (Stern, 1985)

These labels reflect our growing understanding of infant development, and highlight some of the hallmarks of the earliest areas of growth in perceptions of the self. Keep in mind that these stages overlap, with some children making their quantum leaps earlier and some later (see Table 1).

Preattachment and self-regulation. Newborns seem to be innately attuned to people within their environment (Stern, 1985); they are especially attracted to faces. Neonates are capable of imitating facial gestures such as lip protrusions, mouth opening, and tongue protrusions (Meltzoff & Moore, 1977) as well as happy, sad, and surprised expressions (Field, Woodson, Greenberg, & Cohen, 1982). Although it is unlikely that the baby perceives the intent behind the faces, such early abilities demonstrate that babies are highly attuned to facial cues and emotional expressions.

We have long assumed that basic trust is important, but only recently have developmental psychologists examined the subtle, moment-by-moment interactions of mothers and infants (Als, 1979; Brazelton & Als, 1979; Brazelton, Koslowski, & Main, 1974; Chapple, 1970; Sander, 1975; Stern, 1974). They observed cycles of adult's and infant's attention and withdrawal that seemed to serve as precursors of regulation-with-others. Infants' reflexive patterns become organized into increasingly complex interactions with caregivers.

> In an optimal interaction, the reciprocity which is established in these cycles of attention and recovery become the base for affective development, and fuel for [the infant's] learning about the environment. (Brazelton, 1989, p. 420)

Young babies are even known to take initiative in controlling their eye gaze. When observing parents and infants interacting with each other, Stern (1974) and Brazelton and Als (1979) found that babies announced "enough's enough" by averting their gaze, and then looking again into the parent's eyes when they were ready for more. As caregivers feed, diaper, soothe, and play with infants, they are nurturing and shaping children's expectancies about self and others.

The goodness of fit between the child's characteristics and the expectations and demands of the environment are extremely important in the development of constructive relationships (Belsky, Lerner, & Spanier, 1984; Thomas & Chess, 1977). In general, infants who can rely on their caregivers for protection and comfort are more securely attached, which in turn provides a sound base for them to explore the world further (Ainsworth, 1972). We shall see how this process unfolds throughout the early years.

What happens when the child's characteristics fail to match the family's or culture's expectations? Consider a fascinating study involving two groups of infants with irregular sleep-wake cycles conducted by Thomas and Chess (Belsky et al., 1984, pp. 109–110). These low-regularity infants posed a real problem for White, middle-SES families, who demanded regular routines. Puerto Rican parents, who established more fluid family settings, took their infants' low regularity in stride. Such studies alert us to the importance of considering cultural variation in childrearing.

Emerging self. An emerging sense of self also evolves from the very early infant-mother relationship (Bowlby, 1969; Erikson, 1950; Stern, 1985; Sullivan, 1953).

Infants' earliest experiences with others set the stage for their perception of being a self worthy of care. Cuddling while feeding tenderly communicates love and value to a baby; propping a bottle on a cold pillow shouts, "You're not worth my time!"

Babies are also learning that they can trust (or can't count on) those who care for them. Infants whose cries are responded to fairly quickly in the first 3 months of life tend not to cry nearly as much later in their first year (Bell & Ainsworth, 1972). What does that tell us about letting babies cry it out? Not only trust, but children's early sense of efficacy may be endangered.

> Self-esteem, then has its taproot in the experience of efficacy. It is not built merely on what others do or what the environment provides. From the very start it is based on what one can make the environment provide, even if it is only through more vigorous sucking or more loudly sustained cries. In the infant's actuality the feeling of efficacy is regulated by the success or failure of his efforts, for he has no knowledge of what else may be affecting the environment's response. From this point onward self-esteem is closely tied to feelings of efficacy and, as it develops, to the more general cumulative sense of competence. (White, 1963, p. 134)

Feelings of love, self-worth, trust, competency, and even power begin to form long before the child has the capacity to express them in words.

2 to 6 months

Between the ages of 2 and 3 months, the first quantum leap in children's development takes place (Stern, 1985). This change is discernable

The partnership between the child and one or more loving adults is the bedrock of self-esteem.

in encephalographic recordings (McCall, Eichhorn, & Hogarty, 1977). A smile, directed specifically and selectively to the primary caregiver, appears, often as early as one month in well-developing babies. When baby smiles, the response is universal: "How precious!" We smile back at the appealing child. Thus begins the delightful, reciprocal interchange in which parents and other loving caregivers echo and mirror the child's facial expressions and sounds (Emde, 1983).

Once again, various labels have been given to this period of development:

- *Reciprocal exchange,* reciprocity with infant becoming more active, better organized, and capable of coordinating actions with caregiver's actions (Sander, 1975)
- *Attachment in the making* (Bowlby, 1969)
- *Symbiosis,* in which parent and child are seen as intertwined in a mutually need-fulfilling system and from which the baby begins to "hatch" (Mahler et al., 1975)
- *Core self* that emerges through mutual regulation with a "self-regulating other" that enables the infant to demonstrate senses of agency, coherence, history, and affectivity (Stern, 1985)
- *Falling in love* (Greenspan & Greenspan, 1985)

Implicit in these descriptions is the view that parent and child are building an intense relationship as the child's capacities for relationships mesh with the adult's caregiving potential.

The quality of interchanges—tone of voice, nature of touch—constitute the "holding environment" (Winnicott, 1965) that conveys to infants a sense of value and power. Without positive feedback from coos and smiles ("Aren't you wonderful!" "Listen to you sing!") babies become fearful, apathetic, disorganized, and distraught.

Moving illustrations of the flattened affect of two babies whose mothers were depressed, unavailable, and neglectful are described in Fraiberg, Adelson, and Shapiro (1975). Greg, the infant of a 16-year-old, who was at risk for physical abuse, was described at 3½ months as "a solemn baby who never once in that hour looked at his mother" (p. 403). Mary, another baby whose mother's history prevented her from being able to care for her baby adequately, was described in this way:

> At 5½ months she bore all the stigmata of the child who has spent the better part of her life in a crib with little more than obligatory care. She was adequately nourished and physically cared for, but the back of her head was bald. She showed little interest in her surroundings, she was listless, too quiet. She seemed to have only a tenuous connection with her mother. She rarely smiled. She did not spontaneously approach her mother through eye contact or gestures of reach. There were few spontaneous vocalizations. (p. 391)

The "still face" experiments of Tronick, Cohn, and Shea (1984) also illustrate the importance of feedback. When ordinarily attentive mothers were told to stop their usual interactions with their normally developing babies and to assume a still face, the babies became disorganized and upset. They were unable to recover quickly from the event, which was so discrepant with their experience.

However, Tronick (1989) points out that not all parent-child interactions can be perfectly coordinated and that, in fact, there are many disruptions, or *interactive errors* (engendering negative affect), that lead to *interactive repairs* (engendering positive affect). In normal interactions, infants "have a representation of the interaction as reparable and of themselves as effective in making that repair" (p. 116). On the other hand, in abnormal interactions, "With the reiteration and accumulation of failure and non-reparation, the infant develops a representation of himself or herself as ineffective, and of the caregiver as unreliable" (p. 117).

Brazelton and Als (1979) describe four stages of interaction between parent and child: Physiological motor/state regulation, orientation, play dialogue, beginning of object play. These interactions culminate at 4 months in object play, which they believe is the first true test of attachment. At this point, infants begin to move beyond themselves and to explore the world around them. People and objects are fascinating, and the infant's newly developed ability to grasp allows much greater control over how the infant explores.

5 to 9 months

During this period, infants come into their own as intentional partners in truly interpersonal relationships, as these descriptions indicate:

- *Hatching leading to differentiation,* in which the child moves into the first subphase of the separation-individuation process (Mahler et al., 1975)
- *Reciprocal exchange* (4 to 6 months) continues and moves to *initiative* (7 to 9 months) where the infant initiates activities to maintain the social exchange with the caregiver, and selects and manipulates environmental encounters (Sander, 1975)
- *Developing intentional communication,* a period from 3 to 10 months (Greenspan & Greenspan, 1985)

Among the changes that mark this period of development is the autonomous sit (Resch, 1979) that coincides with eye-hand-mouth coordination. The baby can now sit alone in any direction and drink in the personal and impersonal worlds with "a certain new look of alertness" (Mahler et al., 1975, p. 54). Children at this age are far more active, intentional, and outer-directed. Faces of other babies especially intrigue them (Lewis and Rosenblum, 1975). They use their hands and mouths to explore people, toys, household objects, and whatever else is within reach, from dog tails to cups of coffee.

This mother-infant-toys triad is viewed by Stern as a research window through which we can observe the child's developing self-and-others-representations. Among the factors that have been observed are:

- *The provision of toys.* Watson and Ramey (1972) found that infants as young as 2 months show positive affect and try to maintain the stimulation when presented with responsive toys.
- *Maternal behavior used in introducing games* (e.g., tactile, gross body movement, limb movement, visual stimulation, and combinations of these). Crawley et al. (1978) concluded, "the data imply that mothers choose games that will tap infant sensorimotor capacities as well as stimulate positive affect responses" (p. 35).
- *When and with whom the infant imitates, terminates, and thus controls the involvement* (Brazelton & Als, 1979; Lamb, 1977; Power & Parke, 1983; Smith & Daglish, 1977; Stern, 1974; Weinraub & Frankel, 1977)
- *What happens when the environment is bleak, lacking human and inanimate stimulation* (Brown & Helper, 1976; Freud, 1989a; Provence & Lipton, 1962; Spitz, 1946)

From 3 to 8 months, infants take major leaps in self-knowledge as they begin to respond with pleasure to their reflections in mirrors or on videotape (Lewis & Brooks-Gunn, 1979; Papoušek & Papoušek, 1979).

They also have memories, as revealed in an experiment by Nachman and Stern (1983). Babies from 6 to 7 months were introduced to hand puppets that made them laugh by moving, speaking, and playing Peek-A-Boo. A week later, the sight of the puppets alone caused the babies to smile (Stern, 1985, p. 93).

Issues of not only love and trust but also power and competence are firmly entrenched in the child's self-repertoire, long before the first birthday.

8 to 15 months

Attachment and mobility are the hallmarks of this last quarter of children's first year and the beginning of the next. Again, the labels that describe this period are indicative of the changes that are taking place:

- *8-months anxiety,* often termed separation anxiety, indicates the child's strong investment in the primary caregiver (Spitz, 1965). This may appear much earlier in highly sociable, sensitive babies.
- *Focalization,* in which the infant "determines the availability of mother on his specific initiative" (Sander, 1975, p. 136)

- *Practicing,* first crawling and then walking, enabling the child to enter a "love affair with the world" (Mahler et al., 1975)
- *Affective signaling,* rich affective interchanges between infant and another (Emde, 1983)
- Emergence of an *organized sense of self,* a global view that stresses the mutual love affair between parent and child (Greenspan & Greenspan, 1985)
- *Subjective self,* from 7 to 15 months, that consists of *intersubjectivity* ("What is going on in my mind may be similar enough to what is going on in your mind that we can somehow communicate this [without words] and thereby experience intersubjectivity") (Stern, 1985, pp. 124–125) and *interaffectivity* ("The infant somehow makes a match between the feeling state as experienced within and as seen 'on' or 'in' another") (Stern, 1985, p. 132).

Attachment. Researchers have been quite ingenious in creating ways to observe development and relationships in children whose language skills are limited. The *Strange Situation* (Ainsworth, Blehar, Waters, & Wall, 1978) is an attempt to demonstrate the level of security of attachment (avoidant, secure, ambivalent, or disorganized). The child's response to the mother's brief absence, and the child's reactions to a stranger, are measured in this model.

Visual cliff experiments are used to demonstrate interaffectivity (Emde, 1989). Parents are asked to react with expressions of fear or joy, interest or anger when their child reaches the deep side of a table covered with Plexiglas. None of the infants crossed to the deep side from the shallow side if the infant saw a fearful face. Other social referencing experiments also demonstrate the infant's strong affective responses to adults (Emde, 1989; Sorce, Emde, Campos, & Kinnert, 1985).

How parents react emotionally influences how the child responds emotionally to events. A child who falls down may first look toward the parent. If the parent appears anxious, the child will dutifully cry. If the parent responds calmly, the child will brush off the knees and keep going.

Stern (1985) reports experiments in which infants follow the direction of a parent's pointing finger or eye gaze as evidence that the infant has the capacity to respond to another's point of view.

Emde (1983) describes rich communications between parent and child which take the form of

> *affective signaling,* which is biologically based, highly organized, and undergoes development. The infant's signals of distress, smiling, interest, surprise, fear, anger, sadness, and disgust are used for caregiving and are exchanged between parent and infant. In early infancy, such signals predominantly flow from infant to parent, but in later infancy (beginning at 7 to 9 months) they increasingly flow from parent to infant. By the end of the

first year, the infant and another person can communicate about a third event by means of affective signaling. (p. 179) [italics added]

Self-awareness. By their first birthdays, infants are able in a number of ways to demonstrate the dawning awareness of self. Lewis and Brooks-Gunn (1979) note that between 8 and 12 months most infants can associate certain stable categorical features with the self. "Where's your nose?" asks Dad as he bathes baby. And baby puts a finger on the nose.

Thus, the child "can begin constructing the self as a permanent object with enduring qualities" (Damon & Hart, 1982, p. 848). This is consistent with Piagetian theory that object permanence begins to develop toward the end of the first year.

Precursors of empathy are also emerging during this period, especially if empathy has been nurtured by caregivers who display a wide range of tender, loving emotions (Barnett, King, Howard, & Dino, 1980; Hoffman, 1984; Strayer, 1983). At this age, an infant may respond to a playmate's soft whimper upon awakening by rushing to the crib and gently patting the child.

Imitative play is yet another way in which infants demonstrate a beginning awareness of others as apart from themselves. The beginnings of this play include self-pretend acts (pretending to drink from an empty cup), imitation of others (pushing a telephone book in imitation of a parent's vacuuming), and modeling of emotional responses (hugging and making soothing sounds to a teddy bear). This type of play emerges at about 12 months.

By the end of their first year, infants are quite adept at developing action plans and expectancies to guide them in their relations with people. They know which of their behaviors will command immediate attention (spilling a cup of juice) and how beloved parents will greet them when returning from a long day at work (a giant hug and kiss, followed by "Hey, we missed you all day"). Rituals, such as greetings and bedtimes, are established and children expect them to be followed carefully.

Stern's proposals about RIGs (Representation of Interactions which have become Generalized) and Bowlby's working models enable us to better understand how infants are coming to represent self and others. Stern (1985) bases his conceptualization of RIGs on the work of researchers such as Strauss (1979), who demonstrated that very young infants can abstract and generalize from specific experiences.

In describing Strauss's research, Stern noted the infants were shown drawings of faces that differed in terms of placement of eyes or ears or nose shapes. In selecting a single drawing that in essence represented the entire series, they chose "a picture that averaged all the facial feature sizes and placements previously seen, but this 'averaged face' was not part of the series and had not been shown before. The conclusion is that infants have the capacity to aggregate experiences and distill (abstract out) an averaged prototype" (Stern, 1985, p. 98). Nelson and Gruendel (1979) proposed that children as young as two can construct the general sequence of what happens at an event such as a birthday party (arrival, play, cake, presents); they call these *Generalized Event Structures.*

Stern (1985) proposes that episodes of interactions between infant and caregiver involve actions, sensations, and affects, and that "these episodes are also averaged and represented preverbally" (p. 97).

> RIGs can then constitute a basic unit for the representation of the core self. Somehow, the different invariants of self-experience are integrated: The self who acts, the self who feels, and the self who has unique perceptions about the self's own body and actions all get assembled. Similarly, the mother who plays, the one who soothes, and the ones that are perceived when the infant is happy and distressed all get disentangled and sorted. "Islands of consistency" somehow form and coalesce. And it is the dynamic nature of episodic memory using RIGs as a basic memory unit that makes it happen. (p. 98)

Bowlby popularized Craik's (1943) term *internal working model* to describe representations of self and others. Bretherton (1985) defines it:

> Through continued transformation with the world of person and object, the child constructs increasingly complex internal working models of that world of the significant persons in it, including the self (Bowlby, 1969/1982b, 1973, 1980). (p. 11)

As babies begin to develop inner mental structures of meaningful interactions with others, the earliest self appears to be the self-in-action. "I can push the ball!" "I grab Daddy's beard." This characterizes the *sensorimotor period* (Piaget, 1954) that ends roughly in the middle of the second year. Emde (1983) refers to the sense of self prior to 15 months as the *prepresentational self*, built around an "affective core" that provides continuity and organization.

Later, the ability to reflect upon and talk about the self as an entity is the result of developing self-representations that become "inner constructs elaborated during the period of symbolic functioning and capable of symbolic transformations as defined by Piaget (1954)" (Stern, 1985, footnote, p. 49).

Alternate developmental pathways

Culture

The developmental sequences described here and in the following chapters must be weighed in terms of their relevance to our pluralistic world. Damon (1989) states,

As caregivers feed, diaper, soothe, and play with infants, they are nurturing and shaping children's expectancies about self and others.

How a child thinks about and uses an intellectual ability depends on cultural models of competence, while how a child feels about and acts toward persons to whom he is attached depends on cultural models of interpersonal relations. Cultural models of competence and interpersonal relations are, like languages, variables across human populations, creating divergent pathways for behavioral and psychological development of the child. (p. 57)

An example from the attachment research may illustrate this. Secure attachment as defined through American and British populations has been proposed as a requirement for positive emotional development (Ainsworth, 1972; Bowlby, 1969). Yet studies show that in northern Germany, a majority of infants (Grossman, Grossman, Spangler, Suess, & Unzner, 1985) exhibit patterns of avoidant attachment, and in Japan anxious attachment is commonplace (Miyake, Chen, & Campos, 1985). Although it is unclear whether these variations are due to methodological problems or to childrearing differences, they sound a warning concerning the universality of developmental processes.

Undoubtedly, there are many pathways to healthy self-esteem that depend in part on the particular goals and values of the child's culture. As Damon (1989) puts it, "in any given society at a particular time there is an optimal parenting investment strategy for bearing and raising children under the local conditions in which parents can realistically expect to find themselves" (p. 64).

Although we need to appreciate and better understand these local conditions, we need to equally recognize the larger conditions and values that are important for raising children in a modern, democratic, pluralistic, post-industrial society (see the Introduction). Throughout this book we need to combine an appreciation of pluralism with a sense of universalism, concerning the larger common goals. In this regard, we believe that all individuals need a great deal of responsive, supportive adult investment throughout childhood (and even into adulthood) to enable them to construct valued identities in the complex, changing, diverse yet increasingly interactive world in which we live.

Conditions of disability

As indicated earlier, newborns with disabilities enter the world with a variety of conditions that influence their interactions with both the physical and interpersonal environment. Table 2 summarizes the findings of relevant studies concerning disabilities such as mental retardation, hearing impairment, visual impairment, and physical and motor impairments.

The unresponsiveness, the lack of predictable smiling, the inconsistencies in communication, and the flattened affect of some children with

Table 2. Some effects of specific conditions of disability on the interactional skills of children.

Handicap	Reported Findings	Relevant Studies
Mental Retardation	Reduced responsivity to others Decreased vocalization Lack of smiling or delayed smiling More solitary play Fewer initiations to others More likely to resist or not respond to cuddling	Cicchetti & Sroufe (1976); Cunningham, Reuler, Blackwell, & Deck (1981); Kennedy (1973); Marshall, Hogrenes, & Goldstein (1973); Stone & Chesney (1978)
Hearing Impairment	Impaired communication Inconsistent responses to communicative attempts Fewer social initiations	Ferris (1980); Greenberg & Marvin (1979); Schlesinger & Meadow (1972); Wedell-Monnig & Lumley (1980)
Visual Impairment	Irregular smiling Smiling in response to auditory cues only Child must "maintain contact" by tactile and auditory (rather than visual) cues	Als, Tronick, & Brazelton (1980); Fraiberg (1974, 1975); Kastein, Spaulding, & Scharf (1980); Scott, Jan, & Freeman (1977)
Physical and Motor Impairments	Limp or physically unresponsive Difficulty in relaxing Decreased ability to laugh or smile Smile may look like a grimace Impaired communication skills Impaired locomotion skills prevent child from independently seeking out parent	Featherstone (1980); Gallagher, Jens, & O'Donnell (1984); Jens & Johnson (1982); McCubbin, Nevin, Larsen, Comeau, Patterson, Cauble, & Striker (1981); Mordock (1979); Prechtl (1963); Roskies (1972)

From *Teaching Infants and Preschoolers with Handicaps* (p. 148) by D. B. Bailey and M. Wolery, 1984, Columbus, OH: Merrill. Copyright © 1984 by Macmillan Publishing Company. Reprinted by permission.

impairments place extra demands on caregivers who wish to promote interpersonal relationships. This was clearly evident when Curry observed a ventilator-dependent 5-year-old who had been in a hospital respiratory unit since birth. The excellent care she received from doctors, nurses, occupational and physical therapists, and child life specialists is reflected in the fact that she is still alive. However, the lack of continuous caregiving from an invested parent is obvious in her extreme developmental delays and in her apparent attachment to the television set, which has been on all day every day for years. One of the goals of the child life workers has been to try to get her to focus on them, rather than continually turning to the TV set.

Toddlerhood

15 to 24 months

The final quantum leap of infancy propels the child into toddlerhood. Three developmental milestones mark the early period, from 15 to 18 months:

1. Cognitively, children's symbolic knowledge of the world expands greatly, primarily through language and play.
2. Motorically, they become steady walkers who can determine how much distance they will put between themselves and others.
3. Affectively, they strive for independence while still feeling the pull back to dependence.

Theorists apply varying labels to the period of self-development from 15 to 24 months:

- *Autonomy vs. shame and doubt* (Erikson, 1950)
- *Mastery of the No* (Spitz, 1965)
- *Self-assertion* (Sander, 1975)
- *Rapproachement* (Mahler et al., 1975)
- *Verbal self* (Stern, 1985)
- *Emergence of an organized sense of self* (Greenspan & Greenspan, 1985)

Cognitive and motor development. These toddlers are beginning to portray themselves and others in simple episodes of pretend play, as if the distance between self and others is clear enough to begin to experiment (Rubin, Fein, & Vandenberg, 1983). Understanding of what is real and what is make believe is still developing, though. Children from 15 to 30 months "were sometimes confused by their mother's interventions when she joined in their play, even though her support usually led to more complicated play" (DeLoache & Plaetzer, 1985 in Harris, 1989, p. 60).

Their language includes references to themselves and others: I, me, mine, you. Jumping, dumping, and sorting are favorite activities, as they test their motor and cognitive competencies.

By their first birthdays, infants are able in a number of ways to demonstrate the dawning awareness of self.

Affective development. New levels of action and understanding take place, the stage having been set as children increasingly have organized their relationships with others during their first year. Trust has been established, and becomes evident in both their relationships and how they learn through play. "Confidence at the mother's physical and psychological availability appears to lay the groundwork for autonomous exploration and problem solving coupled with the expectation that help will be forthcoming when needed" (Bretherton, 1985, p. 21).

Feelings of love and trust are exhibited in children's sense of competence and control. Children who were rated earlier as securely attached, during this period exhibited more positive approaches to free play and simple assigned tasks (Arend, Gove, & Sroufe, 1979; Bretherton, 1985; Main, 1973). When compared to poorly attached infants, these children had longer attention spans. They appeared confident about solving problems and were willing to ask for help if needed.

On the other hand, 2-year-olds who were ambivalently attached at 12 and/or 18 months were "frustrated, whining, and negativistic" (Bretherton, 1985, p. 20) and were not able to take advantage of adult help even when they needed it. Such children are already becoming powerless to control themselves or their world, or even to rely on the security others can offer.

Self-awareness. The cognitive, motor, and affective developments described here are intertwined with a major advance in children's self-awareness, which is well documented in both the psychoanalytic and developmental psychology literatures. A new reflective self-awareness begins to be exhibited through language and concepts. Children at this age can recognize themselves in a mirror, identify themselves from others in pictures, and categorize themselves by age and sex.

Kagan's study (1981) points out four signs of self-awareness that appear during the months prior to the second birthday: "An increase in directives to adults, mastery smiles, self-descriptive utterances, and distress following the model's behavior" (p. 71). Children frequently became distressed after an experimenter modeled a difficult symbolic act; many of the children responded with crying, clinging, stopping their play, and wanting to leave. "The distress to the model implies that the child has some awareness of his ability, or lack of ability, to meet the standards represented by the model's action" (p. 53).

Erikson (1950) alerted us to the emotional crisis potential of this period with its strong elements of self-evaluations. His description of children's ambivalent struggles with independence are further elaborated upon by Mahler and colleagues (1975), who continue to focus on self issues.

Mahler describes the seeming omnipotence of toddlers which is so easily shattered by their cognitive awareness of separation and feelings of their vulnerability and smallness. Power struggles erupt as toddlers strain to be in control. But sometimes the impossible demands toddlers make may force the adult to take charge. A toddler at a family picnic is the first to be offered a plate of hamburgers, then has a temper tantrum when she can't have all of them.

At the loss of a power struggle, toddlers feel temporarily helpless and deflated. Winning puts them back on top of the world. These swings in feelings about themselves are inevitable in toddlerhood.

For example, Kagan (1981) observed that 18-month-olds anticipated failure. They got upset when presented with a difficult task that was beyond their ability—thus demonstrating a concrete sense of their own competence and inadequacy. Adults must therefore be prepared to assist children as they regulate their self-esteem so that these feelings of allness/nothingness, goodness/badness do not continue to bedevil children.

The push toward independence and all of its heady delights, and the pull back to the comfort of dependency, is wrenching for toddlers, their parents, and other caregivers as well. Some mothers report the "third leg syndrome" in which once free-ranging toddlers become attached to mom's leg, refusing to make forays into the expanding world that were so commonplace just a few days before.

At the same time the toddler begins to demand ownership ("Mine!"), self-control ("Do it myself!"), and to oppose unwanted suggestions ("No!"). Spitz (1965) underlines this third organizer of the ego of this period by speaking of it as the "Mastery of the No."

Although children become more assertive during toddlerhood, it is important to recognize that extreme negativity (the terrible twos) is neither a normal nor healthy developmental pattern. Contrary to the view that children become increasingly negative, evidence shows that toddlers in fact become increasingly self-controlled and less primitive in their non-compliance (Vaughn, Kopp, & Krakow, 1984). Developing compliance and self-control was also related to developmental maturity, particularly language development.

Extreme negativity in toddlerhood appears to be another unfortunate consequence of poor early attachment. In comparison, toddlers with secure attachments have been found to be more adaptable, cooperative, compliant, and likely to have internalized controls (Londerville & Main, 1981; Matas, Arend, & Sroufe, 1978).

Throughout this period, the adult continues to play a key role in shaping the child's view of self. Consider the implicit messages and consequences of labeling children with epithets such as mean, selfish, stubborn, bad, or bull-headed. Or reinforcing only independent or dependent behavior. Or pushing the child away ("You're a big girl now!"). These

The push toward independence and all of its heady delights, and the pull back to the comfort of dependency, is wrenching for toddlers, their parents, and other caregivers as well.

adult perceptions of child — positive or negative — contribute greatly to children's own self-awareness (Mahler et al., 1975). Specific recommendations for facilitating children's development through these sensitive and difficult periods are found in Chapter 4.

2- to 3-year-olds

A number of important developmental achievements intersect during later toddlerhood. Children increasingly shift to symbolic thinking and language during the period from 18 months to 3 years. The remarkable and rapid acquisition of language is accompanied by a consolidation of gains in social, physical, cognitive, and emotional development. Changes in language, dramatic play, and social relations result. Issues of power and autonomy continue in the forefront.

During this time, toddlers consolidate their reflective self-awareness. The growth of this period is characterized by these descriptions:

- *On the way to libidinal object constancy* (Mahler et al., 1975)
- *Recognition* (the ability to use language to describe self, intent, and ideas) and *continuity* (representations of self and others remain continuous, even with disruptions) (Sander, 1975)
- *Verbal self,* in which one's feelings about oneself and others remain relatively constant (Stern, 1985)
- *Creating emotional ideas* (Greenspan & Greenspan, 1985)

Constancy and stability are expressed as children recognize that although their feelings may fluctuate, that they, and the people they love, remain the same. "Sometimes I love Mommy, and sometimes I'm mad at her, but she's still my Mommy."

Woodcock's (1941) classic study of 2-year-olds notes the *process* rather than *product* approach they use in their language, play, motor, and social development. "It is as though he were impelled to make his own life coherent through finding common threads in the multiplicity of experience" (p. 16).

Consolidating developmental gains. For some children, the autonomous struggles intensify well past the second birthday. For others, the urge to define oneself through opposition lessens. Individual differences are clearer at this age than ever before, making it more difficult to generalize about toddler behaviors from research results. For example, in research on social development in 2-year-olds, some authors have found that peer social play increases (Asher & Gottman, 1981; Eckerman, Whatley, & Kutz, 1975; Lewis & Rosenblum, 1975), but others have not been able to document this increase (Bronson, 1975).

Children's play is the perfect window through which to view their growing self-awareness. Woodcock (1941) noted the child's "considerable preoccupation with the topic of himself—especially himself as an actor" (p. 188). Two-year-olds, especially those in groups, seem to go through a stage of commenting on their own actions. "I'm painting." "I'm climbing on the steps!" Conversations between children are peppered with references to "one's self, one's name, one's properties" (p. 189).

Names are the anchor of self. Woodcock (1941) observed 2-year-olds playing a "changed-identity game" in which children exchanged names and roles with one another. However,

> there seems to be a stage in which there is objection to being called by another child's name. The too-immature child ignores it, the mature 3-year-old usually accepts it as a good game and takes it up, often to repeat it to lengths wearisome to adults. Between these two stages seems to lie a period presumably of establishing "Marcia" in one's self, "me," as one and the same, during which period no liberties may be taken with them. (p. 154)

A typical example illustrates how children at this stage respond, even to familiar nicknames. Lathesha, age 2½, had just awakened, and her dad greeted her. "Good morning, Sunshine!" She responded anxiously, "I'm not Sunshine; I'm Lathesha!"

Much of toddler pretend play centers around parental figures and familiar tasks in the home, such as meal preparation and bedtime (Curry & Bergen, 1987). Yet Woodcock (1941) noted that, "In fact, outside of occasional remarks to 'Mommy' or 'Daddy' he does not often address others by name in his play even in functional terms" (p. 230).

Many pairs of 2-year-olds play in much the same reciprocal ways as do older preschoolers. During the second and third years, self-referenced play decreases (feeding oneself out of a pretend cup), while doll-referenced play (feeding a doll from the cup) increases (Rubin, Fein, & Vandenberg, 1983). These play behaviors suggest that the child is viewing the self and others as active agents and experiencers. Similarly, Fein (1984) notes that the child progresses from the self in pretend activities to generic role transformation. Children begin with a single perspective (mother cooking) and then move to a generic role with complementarity and double perspective-taking (mother soothing hurt baby). This awareness of others outside the caregiving circle will flower in the preschool years as awareness and evaluations of self and others become more differentiated.

Consolidating a sense of self. Perhaps the most revealing current research on 2-year-olds is Dunn's (1988a). She studied 55 families and children (ages 12 to 36 months) in their homes. These naturalistic observations, like Woodcock's, yield a rich description of the capacities of

2-year-olds that is often missing in experimental research. Dunn speaks of "the child's developing sense of self in terms of her sense of efficacy and control" (p. 176), and concludes by noting that:

In short, children's curiosity about others' behavior, their interest in approval, disapproval, compliance, and transgression, and their continuing concern with self, together with the frequent attributions, evaluations, and comparisons of family discourse, combine to set the stage for the development of a sense of how others evaluate them. (p. 179)

Harris (1989) reports that very young children have an "imaginative understanding" and appreciation of the mental and emotional states of others. He supports his views with evidence that very young children have:

1. Self-awareness of their own mental states.
2. The capacity for pretense.
3. The ability to distinguish the make-believe from the real world.
4. Understanding of the desires, beliefs, and emotions of others. (pp. 54–55)

Stern's concept of the verbal self meshes with these findings. He notes the importance of being authentic with children. Adult verbal comments and requests should be perceived by children as understanding and extending the children's thoughts and feelings — rather than negating or manipulating them.

Although implications of this research and theory are covered in greater depth in Chapter 4, a few examples are here in order to highlight the importance of the adult role in helping children solidify their sense of self. Children usually demonstrate exuberance about the purchase of a new pair of shoes, are upset by visits to the doctor or dentist, and react with jumping and clapping at the announcement of a birthday party. If the parent reacts by indicating that these intense reactions are inappropriate, the children will learn to subdue other intense reactions in order to please the parent. The danger, says Stern (1985), is that children will present a "false sense" to maintain adult closeness and approval.

A similar danger lies in wait if adults are too intrusive or interpret feelings or motivations to the child that are really the adult's. Commenting, "Oh, my, that block is too heavy for you!" when the child is really testing muscle power in lifting, ignores the meaning of the event for the child. Statements such as, "You just love to share with your little brother" miss the point when the child has just snatched a toy away from the baby.

Already, then, we can see that with the consolidation of the sense of self, children come to feel confident that they are loved and have some control over their lives. We can see how contrasting parenting and teaching styles can lead to different developmental outcomes for children. We move, then, into the next stages of development of self-esteem and beyond.

Chapter 2

Preschoolers: Testing and evaluating the self

WITH THE CONSOLIDATION OF THE SENSE OF SELF, preschoolers begin to test and evaluate that self. Now we can more clearly see the aspects of self-evaluations that Harter has proposed—acceptance, power and control, moral worth, and competence—that serve as organizers for both this chapter and the next.

Preschool children have already developed a variety of physical, emotional, and cognitive skills that will continue to expand and deepen throughout their lives. With good foundations, preschoolers should feel relatively assured that they are lovable and accepted, and they have begun to exercise some power over themselves and their environment.

At the same time, children may be more confident about some aspects of themselves and less secure about others. They may feel accepted by their family, but be less certain about their acceptance among friends. Or they may feel powerful in their play group, but less so at home when they must contend with older siblings. Children's attitudes about one dimension of their development may well affect other dimensions. For example, a child may compensate for feeling unloved by seeking extraordinary power and control.

Children's unique personalities and experiences affect their self-understanding, which becomes ever more complex during preschool years. It could be said that children are developing implicit "theories" about themselves—beliefs about how they usually act, what their preferences are and so forth.

> The self-concept is a self-theory. It is a theory that the individual has unwittingly constructed about himself as an experiencing, functioning individual, and it is part of a broader theory which he holds with respect to his entire range of significant experience. (Epstein, 1973, p. 407)

The skills and confidence that toddlers have developed in their constructive efforts to exercise self-control are now employed to meet new challenges. Preschoolers are variously striving to be *accepted* by friends,

41

helpful to their teachers, *powerful* in their play, and *competent* in their climbing and jumping. Of course, parents, teachers, and increasingly, peers play a central role in both presenting new challenges and providing the support to meet them.

We shall begin by looking at how children's feelings of acceptance — by adults and other children — develop. Then we shall consider the other three dimensions of self-evaluation: power and control, moral worth, and competence, as they blossom during the preschool years. We are guided in this chapter by children's own self-reports, attachment research, and play observations.

Acceptance

Although acceptance is a dominant theme of the infant and toddler years, it remains at the forefront throughout life. All of us participate in the process of building, maintaining, and breaking relationships. Pre-schoolers, whose expanding world includes family, friends, and perhaps teachers, are no exception.

Parents and teachers influence children's self-esteem

Adults continue to play a pivotal role in determining how children feel about themselves and others. Therefore, we must be aware of the effects of various parenting and related teaching styles on the development of children's self-esteem. We shall see how self-perceptions play a continuing role in adult as well as child development, and how this in turn affects self-esteem in future generations.

Parenting styles. Coopersmith (1967) identified three adult factors that specifically enhance self-esteem in children:

- Total or nearly total acceptance of children by their parents
- Clearly defined and enforced limits
- Respect and latitude for individual action within those limits

Research, undertaken in a variety of home, preschool, and laboratory settings, supports Coopersmith's work (e.g., Baumrind, 1971, 1979; Becker, 1964; Hoffman, 1970; Maccoby & Martin, 1983). Children seem to thrive and grow best through interaction with *authoritative* rather than

Self-perceptions play a continuing role in adult as well as child development, and this in turn affects self-esteem in future generations.

permissive or *authoritarian* parents (Baumrind, 1971; 1979). First, we must be clear about the differences in these three styles.

Authoritative: "Firm, loving, and understanding — set limits, but they also encourage independence" (Clarke-Stewart & Friedman, 1987, p. 362).

Permissive: "Avoid laying down rules, asserting authority, or imposing restrictions. They tolerate their children's impulses — children are expected to regulate their own behavior and make decisions on their own" (p. 361–362).

Authoritarian: "Firm, punitive, unaffectionate, unsympathetic, detached, and sparing in their praise" (p. 361).

How are children influenced by each of these styles?

"Children whose parents are *authoritative* are most likely to be friendly, cooperative, competent, intellectually assertive, self-reliant, independent, happy, and socially responsible" (Clarke-Stewart & Friedman, 1987, p. 363).

Children raised *permissively* are likely to be "dependent and unhappy. They are more likely than children with authoritative parents to be outgoing and sociable and to strive intellectually, but these children tend to be immature and aggressive and to lack persistence and self-reliance" (p. 363).

Children with *authoritarian* parents "tend to be suspicious and withdrawn, unfriendly and discontented, well-controlled, fearful, dependent, and submissive, slow to explore and less likely to strive intellectually" (p. 363).

Parents whose children have high self-esteem are clearly concerned about and attentive toward their children. They structure children's worlds along lines they believe to be proper and appropriate. And they permit relatively great freedom with these structures. Acceptance, limits, and respect are also key qualities for preschool teachers (Ayers, 1989).

The attitudes of parents and teachers toward caregiving depends, in part, on how they experienced their own parents. Main's work on parents of children with varying kinds of attachments (Main, 1985; Main, Kaplan, & Cassidy, 1985) lends insights on this issue.

The Adult Attachment Interview was given to parents whose children had been rated in Ainsworth Strange Situation at 12 and 18 months of age. To summarize briefly, parents who were rated as secure valued and reflected positively on their own attachment relationships; had an objective, non-idealized view of their parents and past experiences; and most frequently had secure infants. Parents who were rated as insecure in terms of their own attachment fell into one of three main patterns (Main et al., 1985):

1. Those who tended to have insecure-avoidant infants "dismissed attachment relationships as being of little concern, value, or influence" (p. 91).
2. Those who were most frequently parents of insecure-ambivalent infants, "seemed preoccupied with dependency on their own parents and still actively struggled to please them" (p. 91).
3. Those most frequently parents of insecure-disorganized/disoriented infants, "had experienced the death of an attachment figure before maturity and seemed not yet to have completed the mourning process" (p. 91).

Teachers' childhoods. Teachers' perceptions of themselves as children and their capacities to work with children of different ages have been explored by Rosen (1968, 1972, 1975). She compared teachers' autobiographical accounts with evaluations based on observations conducted by their supervisors.

In one study (Rosen, 1968), first-year teachers were divided into categories of those who were *better-liked* and those who were *less-liked* by their pupils, ranging from kindergarten to the sixth grade, with most in the first three grades. When the evaluations were compared with teacher autobiographies, Rosen concluded, "Thus, while the better-liked teachers expressed enthusiasm for their childhood and a sense of self-esteem about their early lives, the less-liked teachers focused on their past lack of mastery of their world and their uncertain sense of self-worth" (p. 302). Further, the better-liked teachers "conveyed a sense of competence and psychological movement forward in life" (p. 308).

Later, Rosen (1972) studied the relative effectiveness of student teachers with children in three groups from ages 2 through 11. The dominant autobiographical theme for those judged as most effective with the youngest children was a "close and supportive family life in which they had been given a strong sense of love and personal security and much gratification in general" (p. 415). They had not been rebellious during childhood, "underplayed the academic aspects of school experience" (p. 416), and "conveyed a sense of their psychological proximity to their childhood" (p. 417).

The dominant theme of those most effective with the 5- to 8-year-olds "emphasized an early push toward mastery or a precocious assumption of more grown-up roles" (p. 417). Regarding their early experience, "In general, this group either did not focus on past family relationships or described becoming critical and rejecting of their parents' values" (Rosen, 1972, p. 419).

The window of children's attachment enables us to take a closer look at how this process evolves.

Attachment. By the age of 3, according to Mahler and colleagues (1975), children have achieved self- and other-constancy. They can maintain internal images of important others and of themselves. These images remain constant, despite shifting feeling states. Of course, these representations will become even more elaborated and consolidated during the next few years.

Parenting styles, as we have just seen, play directly into children's working models of themselves and others:

> For example, a child who experiences — and hence represents — attachment figures as primarily rejecting, is likely to form a complementary internal working model of the self as unworthy or unacceptable. Similarly, a child who experiences a parent figure as emotionally available and supportive, is likely to construct a working model of the self as competent and lovable. (Bretherton, Ridgeway, & Cassidy, 1990)

Levels of attachment. Levels of attachment in toddlerhood can predict later preschool behaviors and relationships. Children who were securely attached as toddlers attracted more positive responses from unfamiliar peers when they were 3 (Jacobson & Willie, 1986), certainly an important factor for children who encounter new group members in preschool.

Children who were deemed to be avoidantly attached as toddlers, on the other hand, called forth less positive responses when they met newcomers. As preschoolers, they were hostile, restrained, and socially isolated (Sroufe, 1983).

Ambivalent/resistant toddlers became more antagonistic as preschoolers and elicited resistant responses from newcomers (Jacobson & Willie, 1986). Sroufe (1983) found this group of children to be more impulsive, tense, fearful, and helpless.

Researchers have demonstrated that it is possible to study children's internal working models as young as age 3 (Bretherton et al., 1990). They presented open-ended stories, with themes of spilled juice, hurt knee, bedroom monster, departure, and reunion, to children, along with miniature figures, and asked the children to show and tell what happens next. Children were able to understand the major issue in each story and to enact appropriate and different story resolutions.

Specific implications of these findings will be explored in Chapter 5, but we can readily see the influence adults have on children's sense of

Parenting (and teaching) styles play directly into children's working models of themselves and others.

acceptance and their attachment to beloved others. We shall now turn to how children influence each other's feelings of acceptance.

Children influence each other

Friends are increasingly significant in motivating children to modify their behaviors in order to participate in mutually rewarding social interactions. Children's friendships have been studied since the 1930s (Bridges, 1931; Buhler, 1935; Isaacs, 1933). More recently, social psychology researchers have shed new understanding on the importance children have for one another (Asher & Gottman, 1981; Corsaro, 1985; Lewis & Rosenblum, 1975; Rubin, 1980).

Factors that affect early friendships. Although the roots of social interactions begin in infancy, Mueller and Vandell (1979) propose that parent/child relationships and peer relationships follow separate developmental lines.

As we noted in Chapter 1, even infants younger than 7 months of age are especially attracted to images of other young babies (Lewis & Rosenblum, 1975). This attraction to peers escalates through early childhood. Two infants at a family wedding may spot each other from across the room, and then maintain visual contact as they try to squirm away from their parents' arms. Friendships between toddlers are common when children play together in programs and at home.

Very early friendships seem to be based, in part, on familiarity over time (Rubin, 1980) and mothers' liking for one another (Jacobson, 1971). "The most central basis for toddlers' friendships, however, is probably the existence of similarity between their developmental levels, temperaments, and behavioral styles" (Rubin, 1980, p. 25). Physical availability in the neighborhood, home, and preschool is a factor in preschool friendships (Selman & Jaquette, 1977).

Although early friendships are often transitory, close friendships do exist and endure. In carefully observing such friendships, Gottman and Parkhurst (1980) found that young friends were highly sensitive and responsive to each other, particularly in the context of fantasy play. Young friends, more so than older friends, sought to maintain a "climate of agreement" by clarifying communication, sharing viewpoints, and responding to requests. In some cases, such efforts were aimed directly at supporting self-esteem, against feelings of self-doubt, as the following example of the play of Eric and Naomi, two 4-year-old best friends, clearly illustrates:

N. No, it's time for our birthday. We better clean up quickly.
E. Well, I'd rather play with my skeleton. Hold on there everyone. Snappers. I am the skeleton.

E. I'm the skeleton. Ooh, hee . . . Hugh, ha, ha. You're hiding.

N. Hey, in the top drawer, there's the . . .

E. I am, the skeleton, whoa.

N. There's the feet [clattering].

E. [Screams] A skeleton, Everyone a skeleton.

N. I'm your friend. The dinosaur.

E. Oh, hi dinosaur. You know, no one likes me.

N. But I like you. I'm your friend.

E. But none of my other friends like me. They don't like my new suit. They don't like my skeleton suit. It's really just me. They think I'm a dumb-dumb.

N. I know what. He's a good skeleton.

E. I am not a dumb-dumb, and that's so.

N. I'm not calling you a dumb-dumb. I'm calling you a friendly skeleton. (Gottman & Parkhurst, 1980, p. 245)

Similarity, complementarity, and sharing private information are some of the factors that lead to early friendships, according to Rubin (1980). He warns, however,

> Our observations make clear that there is no single basis for children's friendships. The friendships of preschool children — like those of older children and adults — have many functions. Friends can be security givers, standards against whom one can measure oneself, partners in activities that cannot be engaged in alone, guides to unfamiliar places, and apprentices who confirm one's own developing sense of competence and expertise. (p. 69)

Of course, the ups and downs of friendship are a normal part of experience, as are the corresponding ups and downs of self-feeling. Being novices at friendship, 3-year-olds often express concern that "nobody likes me." Children soon learn that recognition one day typically means little the next (Damon, 1988). Unlike children who experience normal ups and downs, children who rarely experience rejection (i.e., overprotected children) are more vulnerable to rejection, whereas children who persistently experience rejection are at risk for numerous psychosocial problems (see Chapter 3).

Values of friendships. Children's ability (or inability) to make friends may reflect their self-esteem, but friendship may also be a means to enhance and refine feelings about oneself. Many upper-middle-SES parents today have one child, or at most two children, upon whom are heaped the hopes, expectations, and indulgences formerly spread across more siblings. Zigler and Long (1986) refer to such children as *gourmet babies,* but even in the 1950s Sullivan (1953) underlined the essential need for peer interactions to help such children become better and more realistically adjusted to everyday life outside the family. Witness 3-year-old David with his close friend, Tony:

(David and Tony are sitting together at the drawing table).

David: "Do you like my drawing?"

Tony: "No."

David: "You have to like it."

Tony: "I don't have to like it if I don't want to."

David: "Why?"

Tony: "I don't like it, that's why." (Rubin, 1980, p. 8)

Children such as David suffer from a too-inflated self-esteem that may lead to the wide fluctuations in self-feelings exhibited by narcissistic adults (Kohut, 1971). These kinds of early down-to-earth experiences with peers are essential to save such children from social maladjustment as they grow up (Rubin, 1980, p. 7).

Children who are neglected, described as the wildflower children by Zigler and Long (1986), also have problems in the regulation of self-esteem. They, too, have social difficulties and are often the ones other children dislike and scapegoat. Such children are hardly likely to get positive feedback from their peers without some adult intervention in appropriate social strategies.

The ability to communicate may also affect whether children are liked by others. Children who are liked talk directly to others, pay attention to everyone involved, respond contingently to and acknowledge the initiations of others, and provide alternative solutions (Hazen & Black, 1989). Similarly, Rubin (1980) described Hartup and colleagues' findings (1967) that popular children "were the ones who most often paid attention to other children, praised them, showed affection, and willingly acceded to their requests," (Rubin, 1980, p. 52). Ricky, at the age of 3, exemplifies this type of child:

> He is an engaging, supportive boy who goes out of his way to involve others in his activities. When Caleb comes out to the big rotating swing, which already has four children on board, Ricky immediately shouts to him, "You can get on it!"
>
> "It's crowded," Caleb shouts back.
>
> In Ricky's view of things, however, there is always room for one more. "Someone else wants to get on," he informs his fellow riders. Then he takes charge of slowing down the swing and shows Caleb where he can climb on. Ricky is a skillful social facilitator, and others like him for it. (p. 52)

Children have a strong need for acceptance and friendship. Indeed, conflicts in preschool frequently revolve around who can play and who cannot. Most of these conflicts are temporary and functional, designed for example to protect ongoing play from disruption (Corsaro, 1985). But children can and do evaluate others and themselves in terms of who is liked and disliked (Hartup, Glazer, & Charlesworth, 1967; Hazen & Black, 1989; Schwartzman, 1978; Sluckin & Smith, 1977). These value judgments may have a profound influence on children's self-understanding: "Even

Children's ability (or inability) to make friends may reflect their self-esteem, but friendship may also be a means to enhance and refine feelings about oneself.

for a 5-year-old, questions of 'Why doesn't he like me?' and its common sequel 'What's wrong with me?' are likely to arise" (Rubin, 1980, p. 79).

Through the window of dramatic play, we find yet another way to view children's self- and other-representations.

Self revealed through dramatic play. Three-year-olds' pretending skills are becoming refined and stabilized, but make-believe play can still be shaky (Slade, 1986). At times the lines between real and make-believe are still fuzzy.

> Three-year-old Johnnie found a Halloween tiger costume in the dress-up corner. He donned it and began to growl menacingly. When the other children ran from this pretend play, he blanched and said nervously, "Take this off me—I can't play anymore." (Curry & Arnaud, 1974, p. 276)

Emotional equilibrium is sometimes difficult to maintain in the face of strong feelings.

Gould (1972) provides a fascinating perspective on how children reveal self-representations in the way they approach play and what roles they choose (nurturer, aggressor, or victim). Themes also suggest what topics are most on children's minds.

> In portraying their view of self and significant others, 3-year-olds, if all has gone well in early childhood caring experiences, engage in nurturing themes of caregiving dyads: Father or mother/baby, nurse or doctor/patient, big sister/little sister, animal/parent/animal/baby. In general most 3-year-olds prefer the more powerful role of caregiver, as if they are still too close to babyhood to perpetuate that status in pretend play. Themes of separation, loss, and return are enacted through roles such as runaway baby or puppy; concerns about the body are depicted in beginning medical play. (Curry & Bergen, 1987, pp. 117–118)

According to Gould, if young children have been poorly nurtured, they often cannot engage in pretend play for one or more of these reasons:

- They become flooded with aggressive imagery
- They may be unable to cognitively distinguish real from pretend
- They cannot take distance from themselves (they become the role, rather than pretend to be the role)

By the age of 4, dramatic play comes into its own. Most children have been engaging in it for 2 or more years, and can now integrate and synthesize a wider diversity of experiences into their play. The dichotomies of good and bad are played over and over, especially in super-hero or TV-based scenarios. (Perhaps this tells us something about adult development in this area as well!)

Differences between dramatic play in 3- and 4-year-old children are beautifully documented in Paley's books (1986, 1988). She writes about 4-year-old Barney, who arrives one morning wearing his dad's Boy Scout shirt and announcing he's going to build a Boy Scout ship.

> "C'mon, Christopher. You can be Batman on my ship," Barney says. "Start building with me."
>
> "I'll do it, Barn," Frederick offers. "Let me be the guard."
>
> Christopher is mobilized to attention. "No, Frederick! No! He asked me *first*. Batman is the guard, didn't you say that, Barn?"
>
> "Two people is okay for guards," Barney adjudicates.
>
> "Then you hafta be a guard, Barn, not Frederick."
>
> "No, Christopher. That's not the way it hasta be. I'm the guy that controls the ship. I shoot the cannons because it was my idea first."
>
> When Barney was three, he did not know "the way it hasta be." He and his friends often sounded like this when they played:
>
> *Barney:* "Emergency! Emergency!"
>
> *Mollie:* "Fasten the seatbelt! Down the bumper!"
>
> Tumbling out of the airplane made of blocks, they would run into the hallway and shout "Emergency!" down the stairs. A moment later the procedure was repeated, this time Mollie yelling "Emergency!" and Barney taking the "Fasten the seat belt" lines. (Paley, 1988, pp. 13–14)

This preoccupation with aggression and power is one of the hallmarks of 4-year-olds, especially boys (Maccoby & Jacklin, 1974; Pitcher & Schultz, 1984). Paley's contemporary year-long recordings overflow with children's preoccupation with these roles, as do Isaacs' (1933) records of nearly 60 years ago. Perhaps 4-year-olds have a firmer sense of who they are, and can now begin to play out the people they would like to become. Like Superman, these children see themselves as accepted, powerful, moral, and competent!

By the age of 4, children's pretend play reveals that they clearly identify with the nurturer, the aggressor, or the victim (Gould, 1972). Cognitively, children can now play out roles with others and demonstrate perspective switching (Fein, 1984). Most make-believe play at this age involves triads: mother/father/child, doctor/patient/nurse, villain/victim/hero. The roles these characters play are also broadened. Parents are not only nurturers, but also go on dates. Super-heroes and glamorous females have great appeal. Table 3 highlights the dichotomy between children whose play indicates a primary identification with a nurturer versus those who identify with aggressors or victims.

The play of 5-year-olds continues to reflect their self-concerns. Play roles expand to include the wider world of industry (firefighter, police officer, astronaut, boss, preacher, even transplant surgeons!) and fantasy (kings, queens, and the ubiquitous super-heroes and TV characters).

Table 3. Dichotomy between preschool children whose play indicates a primary identification with a nurturer versus those who identify with aggressors or victims (Information from Gould, 1972).

Primary Identification With Nurturant Provider	Primary Identification With Aggressor or Victim
1. The child can engage in fantasy. (*Pretends to be* rather than *is* the role.)	1. Child has difficulty engaging in fantasy.
2. The child can distance himself/herself from being the direct agent of aggressive fantasy.	2. Child expresses self directly. Represents the role, rather than *pretending to be* the role.
*3. His/her self-representation is stable.	*3. Roles are unstable and shifting.
4. Self-representation is aligned with the provider.	4. Self-representation is continually aligned with aggressor or victim.
5. Children can maintain a steady stance of pretending and can distinguish between real and pretend.	5. Child shows fluctuating certainty—uncertain about distinction between real and pretend.
6. Fantasy productions integrate the knowledge of the real world with his/her feelings about that world.	6. Child cannot integrate knowledge of real world with feelings about the real world; gets flooded by feelings.
*7. Child has a sense of entitlement. Feels self and others are basically good.	*7. Child engages in global self-condemnation—feels self and others are basically bad.
8. Fantasies are not predominantly aggressive.	8. Fantasies dominated by aggressive themes.
*9. Child has the wish to please others out of love, not fear.	*9. Child behaves in order to avoid punishment.

Note that many very aggressive super-heros have provider aspects (e.g., "I'm He-Man and I rescue people from Skeletor)."

*These descriptions have great relevance to self-esteem issues

Development of the individual self

Now that we are more aware of how adults and children affect the development of self-esteem, we can view the process as it unfolds within the young child through self-understanding and the themes of power and control, moral worth, and efficacy and competence.

Young children's ability to evaluate themselves. Until recently, the prevailing view was that young children were cognitively unable to demonstrate a grasp of an overall concept of self-esteem or its components. In describing the results of her pictured version of the perceived competence scale, Harter (1983) reported, "Not only do young children not possess a concept of general self-worth, but they do not make a distinction between cognitive and physical skills. One is either competent or incompetent across these activities" (p. 331).

However, Eder and Mangelsdorf (in press) document that children as young as three-and-a-half "already have common underlying constructs for organizing information about themselves" (p. 18) such as, " 'When I get angry, I feel like being quiet', or 'When I get angry, I feel like hitting someone'; 'I really like myself' versus 'Sometimes I feel like I just don't like myself' " (p. 61).

During this period, it is also important to help children develop a realistic picture of themselves. Self-feelings should be authentic (Stern, 1985) and lead to an ego that is resilient rather than overly defensive (Block & Block, 1980). Children who are unable to feel bad about themselves—genuinely ashamed or guilty, for example—are surely as disturbed as those who are overwhelmed with such feelings. *Self-esteem* should derive from truly valued actions and standards; *self* should be positively identified with the larger social good.

Growth in social understanding. Preschool children are also developing more sophisticated social understandings. For example, 3-year-olds have an increased awareness of themselves and others as both passive and active agents of self and others behaviorally (mother, father, puppy, baby; as well as categories including age, gender, and race) (Fischer, Hand, Watson, Van Parys, & Tucker, 1984).

Children are particularly attuned to each other's interests and foibles. Paley's (1986, 1988) faithful recordings of the fantasy life of preschoolers bring to life the intensity with which children interact. That children *do* watch, listen to, and recognize what others are into is nicely recorded in this segment:

> One day at snack time Mollie asked Barney if he has his D. "I didn't tell a story today," he answers. The D exists only in stories, but in Mollie's mind it is part of his school persona.
> "We all know Barney's D," I say. "What about Stuart? Does he put something special in *his* stories?"
> "He's a train!"
> "And Mollie?"
> "A ghost and a wolf."
> "Margaret is a kitty."
> "So is Carrie. And William is a bunny."
> "Christopher's an elephant."
> "I'm the Hulk," Frederick says proudly.
> "Erik is good guys and bad guys," Christopher says. "And He-Man."
> The snack table is purposeful and accurate, for it is natural to picture one another in play roles. (Paley, 1986, pp. 63–64)

Children are also keenly aware of status. Corsaro (1985) observed the types of communication children use while playing.

> Overall, the data suggest the children have clear conceptions of status as power. In all the role play episodes, there were no violations of status expectations. That is, the baby never told the mother what to do, the kitties never chased their master from the house, workers never gave orders to the boss. . . . (p. 97)

Preschoolers do, however, have the flexibility to reverse roles (e.g., patient becomes doctor) and thus are able to practice both superordinate and subordinate roles, as they switch perspectives. They are also aware of their own, and others', status. Recall Gould's (1972) findings that children tend to select the role of nurturer, aggressor, or victim. Similarly, Schwartzman's field study (1978) revealed that:

> The roles the children adopt, or are assigned, frequently reflect the authority structure of the play groups . . . and the hierarchy of children outside the play sphere (e.g., those who frequently played "Mothers" and "Fathers" were often the most popular and desired "friends" in the classroom). In house play, the role of pet . . . was generally assumed by one of the more unpopular children in the group. (p. 239)

Danger lurks in this awareness of status and power. Subtly, or not so subtly, sexism and racism can creep into daily life of the classroom, at the behest of either children or uninformed teachers. Boys may be accorded as competent block builders, for example, and thus be permitted to monopolize the block area. Or a minority child might be unwittingly directed toward the role of baby or pet.

Armed with these understandings of self and others, and the cognitive/language abilities to label emotional attributes, preschool children can demonstrate and begin to evaluate how they perceive themselves and others. Their perceptions are limited in part because young preschoolers still tend to view behavior in dichotomies (good or bad, nice or mean), perhaps because that is how behavior is so often labeled by adults. They apparently are unable to understand that there might be reasons for mean behavior, and that these reasons can influence interactions (Fischer et al., 1984). A 3-year-old would not be expected to reflect "If I'm nice to Ana, maybe she won't be mean."

Usually between the ages of 4 and 5, children begin to understand that the same person can be nice one time and mean another, but they still do not fully understand how one individual's nice or mean behavior can influence another's (Fischer et al., 1984).

Self-esteem should derive from truly valued actions and standards; self should be positively identified with the larger social good.

Power and control

We have seen how infants and toddlers begin to exert control over their environment and themselves. Issues of power and control remain at the forefront during the preschool years, demonstrated by two ecological studies of preschool social life (Isaacs, 1933; Corsaro, 1985).

Eder (1989), too, supplies strong support for power as a central aspect of preschoolers' views of themselves and others. *Self-control, general self-acceptance,* and *rejection* appear to be the most salient psychological attributes that three-and-a-half-year-olds use to describe themselves. At the end of the preschool years, five-and-a-half-year-olds focus on *self-control* and *self-acceptance,* achieved now through *achievement* and *affiliation.*

Sex-role development

Dramatic changes take place in children's sex-role development between the ages of 3 and 5. These changes are most evident in the doll-play area. Three-year-old domestic play looks very similar for both sexes, although traditional roles are generally acted out. At 4, many boys rebel and define themselves as super-heroes; many girls manage the home. However, while the text of the play may vary for boys and girls (Teenage Mutant Ninja Turtles; Barbies) the issues of power and control are there for both sexes with girls insisting on the most powerful roles, too (mother, bride, school principal, fire chief).

At 5, Paley (1984) notes that "The doll corner, in fact, is entering its final phase, in which girls and boys try to end lingering confusion about the roles they play" (p. 1). She continues to describe how children's concepts of their sex roles spill over into all areas of the kindergarten classroom:

> . . . You hop to get your milk if you are a boy and skip to the paper shelf if you are a girl. Boys clap out the rhythm of certain songs; girls sing louder. Boys draw furniture inside four-story haunted houses; girls put flowers in the doorways of cottages. Boys get tired of drawing pictures and begin to poke and shove; girls continue to draw. . . . The children watch one another and synchronize their movements. It is the most exciting game in town, though not everyone knows that game is being played. (p. XI)

Many excellent teachers, like Paley, struggle heroically to quell the same-sex play by deliberately providing and reinforcing activities that involve both boys and girls in a wide variety of cooking, construction, carpentry, sewing, and gardening projects. Other more traditional teachers may just go with the flow and unwittingly reinforce gender stereotypes with pictures on the wall (sugar and spice girls, active boys), perpetuating play areas that lead to segregation by gender (a quiet housekeeping corner with all the work props of home versus a vibrant block

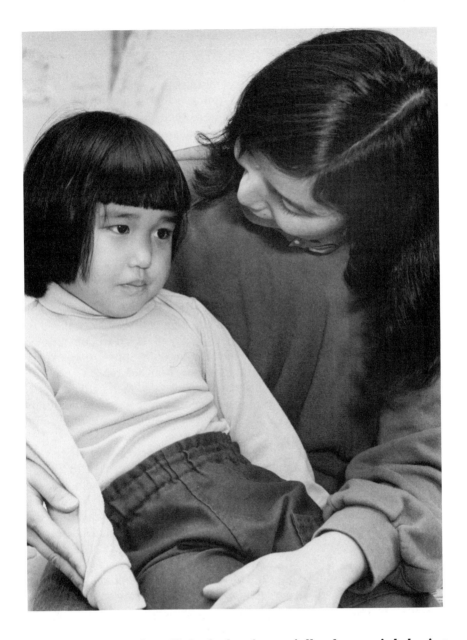

To have the reputation of being bad at 4, especially when one is behaving in an age-appropriate way, can be an ominous foreshadowing of a negative self-image.

corner with wheel toys and wild animals), and even separate special activities (the girls make popcorn indoors while the boys help workers mend the fence outdoors).

Although children may persist in pursuing same-sex play despite these interventions (Paley, 1984; Serbin, Tronick, & Sternglanz, 1977), parents and teachers are encouraged to continue to keep children's options open so that boys and girls feel comfortable engaging in the tasks that most interest them (Derman-Sparks and the A.B.C. Task Force, 1989). Only then can authentic self-development and understanding be realized.

These observations on children's increasing sense of power are intertwined with another critical component of self-esteem in preschool children's development: moral worth.

Moral worth

The gradual shift in emphasis in developmental themes has been well described by Erikson (1950); the psychosocial stage of initiative is at its height in 4-year-olds. Preschoolers view themselves as powerful, competent actors and doers — feelings that can be positive and enhanced by appropriate play and social experiences, many of which will be outlined in Chapter 5 of this volume. These developmentally appropriate experiences enable children to feel virtuous about their behavior.

The negative component of this stage is guilt. Although guilt generally serves an adaptive function as children take appropriate responsibility for their behavior, inappropriate or overwhelming responsibility and guilt is maladaptive.

The labels attached to aggression usually spill over into other children's perceptions of the aggressors, as I (Curry) witnessed in a Head Start classroom. Circle time lasted 45 minutes, by the end of which about five boys began to tussle, punch, and poke. The remainder of the children had simply tuned out. The teacher grew increasingly angry at the bumptious boys and kept uttering threats of the time-out chair. Later, as I sat near a girl who was drawing, I heard her exclaim, "He's bad!" When I asked who was bad, she righteously recited the names of the restless boys from group time. To have the reputation of being *bad* at 4, especially when one is behaving in an age-appropriate way, can be an ominous foreshadowing of a negative self-image. One shudders to think of the children who are labelled in this way, or even more noxiously as *hyperactive,* or having an *attention deficit disorder* (ADD) because of their naturally high activity level.

To demonstrate how such labels ignore the true worth of individuals, let us return to that Head Start classroom as these same boys and I sat together at lunch. John asked me, "Why are you here?"

I responded, "To watch how you play."

Both John and Nick pointed out a fairly new fire engine puzzle and said,

"We'll show you how we put that together." Half an hour later, they went to the puzzle area, pulled out five huge floor puzzles, chose the empty library corner, and set to work showing me how good they were at putting together these intriguing puzzles. The boys called to me occasionally as their work progressed and grinned proudly when the teacher took a picture of them and their work.

These observations poignantly demonstrate how the environment established by adults shapes children's behavior and our perceptions of their actions. These boys, labeled *bad* by teacher and classmates during an inappropriate adult-directed experience, were quite competent to attend to a developmentally appropriate self-initiated task.

Harris (1989) notes children's sensitivities to issues of right and wrong, and stresses that children need to understand the emotional reactions of other children as well as their own. Damon (1988) states,

> As the child's cognitive perspective broadens, it enlarges the sweep of the child's emotional response to observations of others' moral behavior. By early childhood there is a beginning awareness of justice and injustice as regards distribution of toys and other resources in the play group. Soon thereafter develops a sense of obligatory rules and other forms of social propriety. (pp. 27–28)

The research of Smetana (1981, 1984, 1985) demonstrates that preschool children, when told about a child committing several transgressions, were able to judge that moral transgressions (e.g., hitting or stealing) were more serious than conventional transgressions (e.g., school rules about putting toys away). Even abused and neglected children (Smetana, Kelly, & Twentyman, 1984) were able to judge that the conventional transgressions were less serious than moral transgressions. However, preschool teachers responded to both moral and conventional violations, and interestingly were somewhat more likely to respond to conventional violations! (Smetana, 1984).

Harris (1989) states:

> In summary, if we focus not on adult reactions but in the ways that the victims react, young children are offered a clear indication that moral transgressions are more serious than violations of convention: Even if adults make no clear differentiation for the wrongdoer between a moral breach and a conventional breach, other children certainly do. (p. 45)

A fascinating study by Siegel and Storey (1985) notes the importance of preschool experience on children's perceptions of moral versus conventional transgressions. Four-year-olds who had been in school for nine months judged moral transgressions as serious as did children who were only in school for three. The latter, however, took the conventional transgressions much more seriously than did the veteran preschoolers. Thus, teachers need to examine carefully their rule-making, especially in the beginning of school when children are taking to heart so many new expectations.

Table 4. Contrasts in content of high and low self-esteem (Information from Haltiwanger, 1989).*

Key to Self-Esteem Content
Primary defining features: In **boldface** within bars
Secondary manifestations. In *italics*, within bars outlined by broken lines

Dimension: Initiative/Independence

High self-esteem behaviors: (High)

No.	Behavior
9	*Leads others spontaneously*
8	
7	*Ease in transitions, parents to school*
6	Approaches challenging tasks with confidence
5	Sets goals independently
4	Moves forward on his/her own
3	Asserts own point of view when opposed
2	Knows what he/she wants; trusts own ideas
1	Initiates activities confidently

Low self-esteem behaviors: (Low)
- Acts uncertain in making decisions
- Lacks confidence to initiate

Dimension: Preference for challenge

High self-esteem behaviors: (High)

Curious, explores and questions
- Eager to do new things
- Sets high goals; stretches abilities
- Tolerates frustration caused by mistakes
- Approaches challenges with confidence

Low self-esteem behaviors: (Low)

Not curious, does not explore or question
- Gives up easily when frustrated
- Shys away from challenges

Number of items from Q-Sort Criterion Definition

Level of self-esteem:

Dimensions:

Social emotional expression and coping

High

Handles criticism and teasing

- **Adjust to changes and open-endedness**
- **Describes self positively**
- **Shows pride in his/her work or accomplishments**

Hits others aggressively
Has trouble sharing and getting along
Overreacts to stress
Takes more or less blame than reasonable
Has difficulty adjusting to changes
Overreacts to criticism and teasing

Low

- **Smiles infrequently; face often sad**
- **Describes self negatively**
- **Does not show pride in his/her work**

Social approach/avoidance

High

- **Makes good eye contact**

Low

- **Withdraws from group**
- **Hangs back from group; watches only**
- **Avoids eye contact**

(Item content paraphrased)

* This chart is a visual summary of presented self-esteem content for preschoolers, content that was empirically identified in a criterion Q-sort of self-esteem related behaviors performed by experienced preschool teachers. The division of items into "dimensions" was made largely on the basis of conceptual similarities, informed somewhat by patterns of inter-item correlation. Please note that these dimensions and their labels are interpretive and in no way reflect results of any factor analysis or other quantitative criteria dividing content into groups. The division of items into primary features and secondary manifestations is empirically based, however. Primary features performed better on correlations with independent measures of self-esteem, Q-sort and one other independent selection by preschool teachers as central features of self-esteem, and internal consistency measures such as inter-item correlations and item-scale correlations.

Children's reactions to such transgressions involve feelings of pride, guilt, and shame. These emotions inevitably involve children's perceptions about how parents will react (Harris, 1989). He cites Harter and Whitesell's (1989) study

> that children's understanding of pride and shame is indeed linked to the recognition of the impact of an audience. The youngest children (age 4) appreciated that pride was a good feeling and shame a bad feeling, but they could not provide very compelling examples of either. (Harris, 1989, p. 94)

Parents and teachers, however, can provide numerous examples of pride, shame, or guilt. The pride the Head Start children showed in their puzzle-making described earlier was palpable. A child demonstrates shame by facial expressions, turning her back, and flushing when she is chided or when she feels a mistake has been made.

When and how to induce such emotions becomes an important decision for parents and teachers. Too much shame or guilt can strike at children's sense of worth, just as lack of guilt and pride can fuel narcissism. Genuine reflections on both acceptable and unacceptable behavior provide children with a balanced evaluation.

In general, children who have been well-nurtured have

1. A wish to please, not for fear of punishment, but out of love (Gould, 1972)
2. A sense of entitlement and the feeling that they and others are basically good
3. Fantasies, even those aggressive in content, that have a rescuing aspect (e.g., Batman does protect others from the Joker)

As Table 3 indicates, children who have had inadequate nurturing experiences have the opposite characteristics and carry feelings of self-condemnation and badness.

Efficacy and competence

Preschoolers become more involved in an increasingly complicated social world that allows them to test out their self-perceptions. This social world is more easily negotiated by children who have been developing a sense of efficacy from birth.

> From this point [infancy] onward self-esteem is closely tied to feelings of efficacy and, as it develops, to the more general cumulative sense of competence. It is constantly undergoing modification as the child directs his effort toward manipulative activity, locomotor accomplishments, mastery of language, and assertion of his desires with respect to others. It moves up and down as social roles are tried out and as identifications are attempted. (White, 1963, p. 134)

Dunn (1988a) reminds us of Harter's view that the child's sense of "efficacy and control is a critical dimension of self-evaluation" (p. 177). She feels that a major task for children during their third year is to learn "how to manage their social world. A child's sense of self-efficacy is likely to come, then, in large part from solving these problems, from having control over such social matters" (p. 177).

Three- and four-year-olds who have opportunities to play with others have had practice in social problem solving and feel confident about their skills in this area. Threes demonstrate fairly subtle self-understanding. Fours display more complex representational structures, as exhibited by their play that centers on power and aggression.

By the age of 5, children's competencies are manifold: their play roles reflect their awareness of the wider world beyond home and family (Arnaud, 1972), their social skills are becoming more refined, and their cognitive capacities enable them to integrate and synthesize much more of their experiences than they could even a year ago.

Emotionally, 5-year-olds are just beginning to explore a new era in terms of the self-view (see Chapter 3). Erikson (1950) speaks of the *industry* of school-age children, with the concomitant danger of feeling *inferior* if they cannot meet the challenges school and society place on them.

Most 3-year-olds are uncritical of their art projects, block constructions, and play scenarios. Five-year-olds, on the other hand, are much more aware of other children and how they compare to one another. The former slap-dash, can-do attitude of younger preschool children gives way to a more cautious self-monitoring by the time children reach kindergarten age. When confronted with a new challenge, children who are confident generally tackle the task eagerly. Those whose sense of competence has been undermined may give up, refuse to try, or resort to bombastic boasting ("*I* know how") when confronted with some new challenge.

Table 4 presents a useful survey of the behaviors of children with high and low self-esteem as established by Haltiwanger (1989). Her study undertook to identify the classroom behaviors associated with self-esteem of preschool children, based on the judgment of experienced preschool teachers.

This review of research on the development of children's self-esteem and beyond contains many implications for parents and teachers, from interaction styles to play area design. Readers eager to see how the principles elaborated upon here can be applied to everyday living will find direction in Chapter 5.

As the preschool years come to an end, children reach yet another turning point in their lives. They begin to set new standards of self-evaluation, as we shall see in Chapter 3.

Chapter 3

Kindergarten and primary children: Setting new standards for the self

BY ALL ACCOUNTS, THE EARLY SCHOOL YEARS MARK a major turning point in children's lives. They are a period of dramatic change, psychologically and socially, that ends with the beginning formulation of a new understanding of self.

- Cognitively, children are developing new ways of thinking about themselves and others. These changes are associated with their entry into what Piaget (1952, 1954) has termed *the stage of concrete operations.*

- Emotionally, children are entering the period Erikson (1950) described in terms of *industry* versus *inferiority.* Feelings about self are increasingly dependent on children's success in participating in productive tasks and relationships outside the home.

- Socially, children experience themselves in new settings with new tasks, responsibilities, roles, relationships, and evaluations (Higgins & Parsons, 1983).

- Physically, children are highly active, yet increasingly coordinated and controlled, as they participate in games, dance, and sports.

As always, self-esteem in the primary years depends on many factors that make up the fabric of children's lives. Their world expands to include an enormous variety of new social contexts. With increasing autonomy, depending on interests and opportunities, children venture into neighborhoods, sports, scouts, camps, hobbies, and lessons of all kinds.

The breadth of this social world extends well beyond the scope of this chapter and often beyond the current scope of research. Experience tells us, however, that for many children such outside activities play a central role in their lives and identity. Some children live for sports, others find important identities and competencies in music lessons or clubs. In fact, parents and their children are sometimes far more deeply engaged in these social groups than in school. We also know that churches and other neighborhood organizations often have played a critical role in giving direction and hope to children in poverty (Heath, 1989). All children need a variety of opportunities to explore individual interests and engage in valued pursuits.

Against this variety of socializing agents outside of the family, the school stands out as the only mandatory context deemed to be of universal value. No other institution has the potential for such general impact on children's lives and sense of self. Regardless of a child's economic, racial, or family background, schools potentially give all children the opportunities to be engaged in a socially and personally valuable enterprise. We know most about children's lives in school, and can potentially do the most to make positive changes there. Hence, we will focus primarily on self issues as they appear in the context of school, recognizing that these issues extend to other contexts as well.

Adjustment to formal schooling will depend upon how individual characteristics of the child fit with the particular demands of the school environment. Understandably, children who have suffered persistently inadequate parenting and/or nonsupportive preschool environments may suffer, both from negative self-representations (Cassidy, 1988) and from less adaptive patterns of behavior. Attention span, persistence, ego resilience, and social functioning in school have been linked to children's earlier social experiences (Bretherton, 1985, p. 21). Whether these deficiencies will be further aggravated or ameliorated will depend upon how well the school environment supports further development.

As with all major life transitions, the early school years mark a period of increased risk as well as opportunity (Sugarman, 1986). The new demands of school challenge children's abilities to adapt. Although most children experience only temporary difficulties in starting school, a minority of children fail to adjust, and they deteriorate during the first 2 years (Dunn, 1988b). Such failures may be internalized in negative attitudes toward self and school, leading to a continuous cycle of maladaptive behavior and further failure. For others, the early school years may provide an opportunity to break negative cycles and establish new, more positive life trajectories (Rutter, 1987). For some students, who suffer in negative family environments, school may provide a new arena of relationships and success, supporting a more positive identity.

Developments in the primary school years are marked by one common theme: Children are coming to evaluate themselves according to new standards. In part, these standards are imposed by new demands. Teachers, parents, and peers alike expect and encourage school-age children to be more grown-up, autonomous, responsible, task directed, and self-controlled. And there are new tasks and measures of competence, particularly academic tasks and grades.

Yet, there are equally powerful changes coming from children's own changing view of themselves. Children typically value their new identity as school children and quickly internalize new standards of maturity. Moreover, children are developing new abilities that enable them to function and evaluate themselves in new ways. Particularly central is the development of the ability to explicitly compare self to others. Children increasingly evaluate themselves in terms of how they measure up, bringing a new risk of inferiority, as Erikson (1950) aptly described it. These new standards of evaluation are evident in each component of self-esteem: In children's sense of self as being *competent, powerful, accepted,* and *virtuous.*

Competence

Expectations and beliefs about academic success

A popular idea arose in the late 1960s: If individuals believe they will be successful, they will in fact be more successful. The so-called Rosenthal effect, or self-fulfilling prophecy, was based on research purporting to show major effects of teacher expectations (Rosenthal & Jacobson, 1968) and quickly became a part of professional folklore.

As nice as this ideal is (like Peter Pan, if only we believe . . .), more careful reflection and research shows that expectations neither simply nor directly predict performance, particularly in the early school years. Those first studies were criticized as flawed (Elashoff & Snow, 1971), but subsequent research provides a more complicated picture. Although beliefs and expectancies are certainly important, they must be viewed in connection with actual characteristics of children (see Figure 1 in Chapter 1).

Children's beliefs. Numerous studies have demonstrated that, for the most part, young children are exceedingly optimistic in self-ratings of their abilities and expectations for academic success (see Licht & Kistner, 1986, and Stipek & Mac Iver, 1989, for reviews). Not surprisingly, as children are first initiated into the world of school tasks — reading, writing, and arithmetic — they have little clear idea of what their competencies will prove to be.

As children get older and become more experienced, their initial optimism gives way to increasing realism. The reality is that there are differences in abilities and levels of achievement. The adults' task is to help children understand that although not everyone can be super-skilled at everything, all children can feel OK about their present abilities and positive about their prospects for improvement.

Billy, a Native American, began school with all the enthusiasm and optimism of a first grader. Despite living in urban poverty with an

The best predictor of school performance is not children's self-expectations, but rather their social-emotional maturity.

alcoholic mother, he was excited about being a big boy, learning how to read and write. He did his best, despite his limited resources. But within a year his frustration became overwhelming and his enthusiasm waned. He complained that "My teacher says I can't do good work." Billy's teacher destroyed his sense of competence by failing to appreciate and support his efforts.

Children begin the school years with very global, undifferentiated ideas of their abilities. Their concept of *smart,* for example, does not refer to intellectual ability alone. Being smart includes being *nice, well-behaved,* and *hard-working.* Other research demonstrates that children at this age also tend to see cognitive and physical abilities as being related to a single general notion of competence (Harter, 1990). In addition to being relatively undifferentiated, children's self-evaluations are also relatively nonintegrated. Harter (1990) finds that children of this age are unable to consciously evaluate their sense of self-worth as a whole. Hence, as children enter the school years they have little explicit understanding of their distinct talents, either alone or in combination.

In some ways, the limited understanding of young children is an advantage. Children do not begin school with preconceived notions about any limitations in their intellectual capacity. Instead, as Dweck and Elliot (1983) explain it, children initially view ability as an *incremental process,* not as a *fixed entity.* Young school-age children assume thay are smart because they believe their efforts will pay off in incremental improvements: They are growing bigger, better, smarter, and stronger.

Experimental studies have similarly shown that young children's expectations are comparatively resistant to evidence of failure. Children in the early school years are less likely to conclude that poor performance on a task implies something about their ability to perform in the future (see Stipek & Mac Iver, 1989, pp. 524, 526, 528). As children get older, however, they come to realize that effort is constrained by ability.

Although the data suggest that young children are less vulnerable to negative views of their ability, they are not immune (Licht & Kistner, 1986). Some children express globally negative views of themselves; others vacillate between extremely positive and negative self-appraisals (Harter, 1977). Young children's overt, verbal optimism may overlook or belie a more covert pessimism, evident in their lack of initiative and persistence, as well as more specific self-assessments (Eder, 1989; Stipek & Mac Iver, 1989). And excessively high self-ratings may be defensive reactions against deeper feelings of inadequacy: Abused children have been found to be more optimistic than nonabused children (Vondra, Barnett, & Cicchetti, 1989); lower-SES minority children have been found to be more optimistic than higher-SES children (Entwisle & Hayduk, 1982).

Hay (1989) found that children who judged themselves perfect on a measure of self-esteem tended to be otherwise highly vulnerable, defensive, and preoccupied with gaining external approval and avoiding social rejection. Among older grade-school children, Connell and Ilardi (1987) found that children who over-rated their competence (compared to their actual performance) were judged by teachers to be less self-directed than under-raters and were more motivated by fears of failure than by intrinsic desires for success.

Consider the case of Annie, studied for several years by Campbell (1990). Beginning in Annie's infancy, her mother was extremely negative and insensitive. The mother perceived her daughter as being exceptionally difficult. But Annie's behavior did not live up to her mother's image. On the contrary, in school Annie was described as being very sociable, cooperative, attentive, and successful academically. In fact, Annie's adaptive behavior was driven by a tremendous need for support and attention, reflecting a highly vulnerable sense of self.

In addition to their overt optimism, some children entering school may bring with them covert attitudes and behaviors that interfere with actual achievement. In this light, Alexander and Entwisle (1988) found that the best predictor of actual school performance was not children's self-expectations, but rather their social-emotional maturity: "Children who have the ability to postpone gratification, to be socially responsive in appropriate ways, to maintain control over their emotions and to be in a positive frame of mind apparently profit more from early schooling" (p. 104). In Erikson's terms, psychosocial immaturity may be characterized by a lack of *initiative* which may now interfere with the development of a sense of *industry*.

Research on the enduring consequences of mother-child attachment relations points to two developmental pathways that place the self at risk. Children with ambivalent, resistant relationships may, like Annie, exhibit an adaptive but vulnerable and dependent sense of self. Children with avoidant relationships, on the other hand, suffer from more seriously maladaptive problems. They tend to avoid and express hostility toward others, and lack motivation for achievement (Bretherton, 1985).

Children's developmental levels. Children entering kindergarten and first grade exhibit a broad range of developmental levels. Some are more able than others to function successfully within the traditional framework of school expectations.

However, rather than revise curriculums and behavior expectations to address this typical variation in children's developmental levels, most school systems have tried to find ways to make children fit the system (Bredekamp, 1987, 1990). Policies designed to give children time to get ready include raising kindergarten entrance ages, holding children out for another year before kindergarten, having children repeat kindergarten, or assigning less mature children to an extra year before first grade in what have been termed developmental, transitional, or kindergarten readiness programs.

On the surface, these policies and programs appear to be developmentally appropriate. But they are not effective (Peck, McCaig, & Sapp, 1988), and most of them place children's self-esteem at great risk. Shepard and Smith (1986) summarize the research on why such efforts fail to meet children's developmental needs:

On being youngest. Children who are youngest in their first grade class have slightly lower achievement rates, but the difference is only 7 to 8 percentile points, and disappears by about third grade. Schools should reexamine their referral and retention practices if they find that the majority of targeted students are the youngest in each grade. Unwarranted referral or retention may have negative effects later on.

On entrance-age policy. Kindergarten entrance age has increased gradually over the past 30 years. A child who was among the older students in class in 1958 would today be one of the youngest. In most states children have to be five years old before 1 October to start kindergarten. Regardless of the entrance age requirement, however, the youngest children are *always* at a slight disadvantage. Thus, raising the entrance age is a temporary solution to a problem that is relative rather than absolute.

On voluntarily waiting a year to start school. Many parents are choosing to keep their children out of school an extra year so that when they do start school, these children will be in the less at-risk group of older students. These children may, however, eventually be insufficiently challenged. Furthermore, schools should not encourage parents to keep their children home because this policy invariably increases students' age differential in kindergarten and first grade.

On assessing children's readiness for school. Many of the tests being used to place and evaluate children were designed for other purposes, such as helping teachers plan instruction. None of the available tests is accurate enough to screen children into special programs without a 50 percent error rate.

On kindergarten and first grade retention. By the time they complete first grade, children who have repeated kindergarten do not out-perform comparison students; they do, however, have slightly more negative feelings about school. There is no achievement benefit in retaining a child in kindergarten or first grade and, regardless of how well the extra year is presented to the child, the child still pays an emotional cost. (p. 80)

Transitional programs are now illegal in California (Brewer, 1990). Some extra-year programs may be developmentally appropriate, but others are not (Bredekamp, 1990). Even with the best of extra-year programs, all too many school systems put most of their young children in boring, stressful kindergartens and first grades.

Bredekamp (1990) challenges us to think of the long-term implications of these programs as well. Some children could take as many as four years to finish first grade. At the other end of the public school spectrum we will find seniors who graduate (if they don't drop out first) at the age of 20.

The sad fact is that even the best extra-year programs only serve as a disguise for the real problem: inappropriate kindergarten and primary curriculums. We must work together to make children's early elementary years as supportive of their development as we know how to do.

Expectations of children with various learning impairments. What about the self-perceptions of children who suffer from genuine impairments or limitations in academic competencies? Generally speaking these children, like all children, develop increasingly more realistic and differentiated concepts of their abilities. In the later school years, for example, children with specific learning disabilities come to differentiate their different strengths and weaknesses, although it appears that children with problems in reading are more likely to overgeneralize their beliefs about themselves as readers to other areas of competence (Licht & Kistner, 1986). Children with specific learning disabilities also come to evaluate themselves differently according to different reference groups. They feel less competent among their nonimpaired peers and more competent among other children with specific learning disabilities (Renick & Harter, 1989). Children with mental retardation, on the other hand, come to understand their condition as being more general, and they identify more exclusively with other children who are mentally retarded (Licht & Kistner, 1986).

Problems do not lie in the fact that children conceive of themselves as in some ways less able, but in the meaning adults apply, and children come to accept, about such conceptions. Some children and their teachers treat their limitations as a passive state that must be accepted, whereas others treat them as an obstacle to be overcome.

In general, children with specific learning disabilities have been found to be at risk for the more passive attitude: They are less likely than their nonimpaired peers to take credit for their successes. They tend not to see their difficulties as changeable (a likely reflection of their experiences in the passive, rote-learning environments common in special education). Such attitudes are not inevitable, however. Some children with specific learning disabilities persist despite repeated failures, convinced that their efforts will eventually pay off (Covington, 1987).

Children with mental retardation are similarly at risk. Weisz, Bromfield, Vines, and Weiss (1985) found that the label *mentally retarded* tends to lead adults to focus on children's lack of ability, at the expense of emphasizing their potential for effortful change. Although these children do have limitations, emphasizing their limitations may lead to a sense of helplessness that further lowers their potential achievement.

Parent expectations. For the most part, parents also have high expectations for their children's abilities and success in school. These expectations may or may not be related to children's success.

Contrary to some stereotypes, parents of lower-SES minority families do not hold lower expectations for their children. In fact, when Stevenson, Chen, and Uttal (1990) interviewed 1,000 mothers and their children, they found a

> greater emphasis on the concern about education among minority families than among White families. Black and Hispanic children and mothers evaluated the children and their academic abilities highly; they were positive about education and held high expectations about their children's future prospects of education. (p. 508)

Other research suggests that such optimism may be particularly fragile, however. Alexander and Entwisle (1988) found that grade-level retention had a much more prominently negative effect on African American parents' views of their children's abilities than on White parents' expectations.

Although we do not fully understand these effects, it may be that many parents, especially those with fewer years of formal education, have difficulty in accurately assessing their children's abilities. Both parents and children are initially hopeful during the early elementary years, but are also more readily crushed by evidence of failure. These parents may also be less sensitive to the kinds of support or scaffolding of experiences their children need to continue to achieve. Hence, their hopes may not be supported by plans for their realization.

School and teacher influences. The development of children's understanding of intellectual competence is not simply a matter of cognitive maturation. Generally speaking, children adapt their self-understanding to their teachers' expectancies and behaviors (Higgins & Parsons, 1983; Stipek & Mac Iver, 1989).

Children begin elementary school with little understanding of academic competence in part because preschool life appropriately offers them little opportunity to single out, test, and compare their performance on academic tasks. Preschool teachers typically give children positive feedback for individual efforts, and rarely criticize or compare children's accomplishments.

In most cases, children are gradually exposed to the rigors of formal education during the early elementary years. Observational studies indicate that at first teachers particularly emphasize children's acquisition of the student role. They socialize work habits, respect toward teachers, and cooperation with peers and deemphasize academic performance. Even when assigning grades, teachers' assessments in the early years may be greatly influenced by student conduct. Even written reports to parents often contain as many or more assessments of children's conduct as they do of children's academic progress.

It is little wonder, then, that children also include social behavior, work habits, and effort in their definitions of being smart. When viewed from this perspective, it is easy to see why young children find extrinsic motivators such as praise or stickers—indicators of teachers' general approval—so appealing, as opposed to more objective and specific feedback.

The later elementary years are characterized by increasingly standardized school tasks, objective assessment, and competitive activities that set the stage for academic comparisons. Moreover, the amount of positive reinforcement declines as teacher-pupil relationships become less personalized and more focused on teaching and learning (Stipek & Mac Iver, 1990).

These findings demonstrate that teachers are generally sensitive to the developmental needs of young children. Teachers of young children emphasize the gradual socialization of children into the more formal learner role, stressing the importance of the *process*—hard work and cooperative behavior—over the *product*—grades and competitive comparisons. In this regard, many of the most serious risks of formal schooling await the later school years, as children increasingly focus on their relative abilities in increasingly competitive and impersonal environments. Nonetheless, early education often still leaves much to be desired.

While we can take heart in the fact that teachers are sensitive to developmental characteristics of young children in general, we also know that there is much room for specific improvement. For example, school officials and teachers appear to place too much weight on age in assessing children's developmental levels, and they too readily mislabel immature children as learning disabled (Shepard & Smith, 1986). Schools may also underestimate the potential of children who are labeled mentally retarded. In other cases, we know that teachers push formal academics too early and too hard.

In general, concerns about early education fall into three camps: Academic goals in early childhood are viewed as too demanding, too lax, or too insensitive. **In the first case,** early childhood educators have been particularly concerned about the dangers of pushing young children into formal academic learning. Elkind (1981) has warned of the consequences of the hurried child, which among other things includes pushing children too early into formal education. Recent research has suggested that early

School learning and competence will be best facilitated when children are engaged in active, meaningful, goal-directed cognitive enterprises.

formal schooling appears to offer no advantages while entailing risks for increasing competitiveness, negative attitudes toward school, and decreased creativity (Hirsh-Pasek & Cone, 1989).

Early academics are also known to spur children's ideas about their comparative academic abilities (Stipek & Daniels, 1988), with the attendant risk that children will draw premature and erroneous conclusions about their talents and abilities. For example, if the tasks are too abstract or require quiet sitting, children can easily conclude that they are not very good learners. Such risks are compounded because children will recognize that they have failed to meet their teachers' expectations.

Although it is a mistake to push academics too hard and too soon, particularly in the preschool years, **our second concern** is that it seems to be equally a mistake to push academics too little and too late. In fact, the most serious problem in the primary school years is that children are challenged too little.

Kindergartens that take a whole year to teach the alphabet, counting, shapes, and colors with worksheets are exceedingly boring and inappropriate for all children. These programs are especially a waste of time for kindergartners who can already write their names, recognize a few words, count, know how to use shapes, and select vibrant colors in creative art experiences. We do not mean that young children need more formal drill. What they need is more elaborate scaffolding of exciting, developmentally appropriate educational challenges, such as those young children increasingly experience during the preschool years.

The evidence suggests that after children begin elementary school, Americans are anything but pushy when it comes to education. Stevenson and Lee (1990) found that Minneapolis mothers, as compared to mothers in Taipei, Taiwan and Sendai, Japan, were more accepting of any level of effort and less involved with their children's academic achievements. In turn, children's academic self-concepts were so unrealistically positive that Stevenson and Lee (1990) were left wondering whether such beliefs might prevent children from recognizing the need for hard work.

The third concern is that education is too insensitive to children's needs. Research has consistently shown that the typical American elementary school classroom is remarkably rigid and insensitive to child characteristics, whether they be individual (Gardner, 1983), developmental (Resnick, 1989), or cultural (Heath, 1989). School life is still reminiscent of factory life in the 19th century: Like the isolated factory worker carrying out orders from a superior, children are taught to follow directions and work on their own (Graff, 1979). This structure not only ignores cultural backgrounds that stress cooperative goals (Tharp, 1989) but also neglects to teach children skills of collaboration and negotiation so important in modern life (Heath, 1989).

Even more disturbing, such school experiences very likely give children the wrong ideas about themselves as learners. Learning is presented as a passive activity in which teachers supply information and students accept it, rather than something children actively do through their own intellectual and social activity (Greeno, 1989). In this context, children's intrinsic motivation for learning typically declines during the grade school years (Harter, 1983), and children may be inclined to view their intellectual ability as a passive trait, rather than as an active process (Dweck & Elliot, 1983).

In sum, we believe that children's sense of competence in school will be facilitated best when they are engaged in active, meaningful, goal-directed cognitive enterprises. High expectancies are not enough. Educational goals must be adjusted to individual differences in abilities, with support provided to ensure success. The objective is to ensure that children experience genuine success that derives from committed efforts toward achieving highly valued goals.

It is a mistake to present learning as primarily a formal, impersonal, passive activity. Yet it is equally a mistake to dismiss academic learning in favor of curricula with ill-defined goals. Children need to learn about the wonders of learning and the value of using one's head in the pursuit of individual and social goals. We need to "engage children's minds," as Katz and Chard (1989) so aptly put it, in meaningful goal-directed projects in pursuit of explicit educational goals.

Power

Rothbaum and Weisz (1988) have described middle childhood as the "age of power," a period in which children are increasingly concerned with their status as compared to others. Just as children are coming to measure and scale the physical world, so too are they measuring and scaling the social one.

Although children are becoming increasingly comparative and competitive in their social judgments, it is important to recognize that status with others is not the only route to achieving a sense of power. The alternative is an inner sense of power and control that comes from directing one's own behavior, accomplishing one's goals, and expanding one's skills. This includes the sense of an internal locus of control and self-effectance (Bandura, 1986), and the belief that personal effort will be rewarded ultimately. Children with this sense of internal power have the confidence to persist despite repeated failure.

Both of these senses of power are developing in middle childhood, but individuals and classrooms differ in their emphasis (Nicholls, 1990).

Some children and classrooms are measurably more inner directed and *task oriented,* concerned about expanding children's knowledge, skills, and understanding as fully as possible. Others are more externally directed and *ego oriented,* focused on children's relative status compared to others. Ego orientation is associated with beliefs that success in school depends upon being superior and beating others. Task orientation, in contrast, "is associated with beliefs that academic success depends on interest, effort, collaborating with others, and trying to understand rather than just memorize" (Nicholls, 1990, p. 37).

These findings indicate that *perceived academic ability* need not, and should not, be viewed as the sole determinant of either academic success or self-esteem. Not all children can be superior academically, but all students can come to appreciate themselves as learners: "Students who believe they are low in ability relative to their peers can nevertheless be highly oriented to understanding and working hard in order to learn" (Nicholls, 1990, p. 37).

Of course, most good elementary teachers discourage ego-oriented competition and comparative judgments, preferring to reward task-oriented effort and cooperation (Covington, 1989). But it is difficult to resist larger cultural and social forces that emphasize competitive achievement. The reward structure of school, emphasizing grades and comparative standing, often has a dominating influence. Even subtle comparative comments (Heckhauser, 1984) or a small number of competitive, ego-oriented children can disrupt task-oriented behavior. To resist these pressures, Covington (1989) insists that "teachers must actively restructure classroom incentives to encourage other more beneficial reasons for learning" (p. 98). Models for such a restructuring will be discussed in Chapter 6.

Of course, there is no way to escape the fact that all children have different abilities. Nor are all social comparisons and competitions necessarily evil. Children need to develop an honest appraisal of their strengths and weaknesses, and competition can function positively to stimulate achievement. The point, simply, is that an individual's relative abilities should not be the primary basis for self-evaluation or receiving rewards. The dominant ethos of the elementary classroom should be cooperation and attention to tasks, with social comparisons and competition serving subordinate functions.

Negative effects of ego-oriented power also show up in behaviors such as bullying, scapegoating, and victimization. As they become more sensitive to their relative social status, children in the middle years increasingly employ strategies and defenses to enhance and protect their egos. Thus, both males and females who feel put down may seek to build themselves up by putting others down. As Olweus (1978) describes it:

Not all children can be superior academically, but all students can come to appreciate themselves as learners.

For a boy with bullying tendencies, the potential whipping boy is an ideal target. His anxiousness, defenselessness, and crying give the bully a marked feeling of superiority and supremacy, also a sort of satisfaction of vague revengeful impulses. (p. 142)

Both the perpetrator and victim commonly suffer from the same self-defeating ego orientation. Instead of focusing on the constructive tasks of building, maintaining, and breaking social relations, such children focus on their own relative power and status. Whereas the victimizers obtain a temporary sense of power at the expense of others, the victims may also gain a sense of power by inviting abuse, intentionally becoming the scapegoat or butt of humor (Rothbaum & Weisz, 1989).

Acceptance

School-age children are both nicer and meaner than their preschool counterparts. They are nicer in that they engage in more sharing and altruism, with fewer quarrels and physical attacks. But they are meaner in that they increasingly deploy insults, derogation, and other threats to self-esteem. Whereas aggression among younger children is relatively more *instrumental,* directed toward retrieving objects and the like, the aggression of older children is more *hostile,* directed at the person and his ego (Hartup, 1974).

Kindness and hostility go hand in hand as children exercise their growing abilities to understand and affect the feelings of others. Children who are highly prosocial are often the same children who are tactically hostile. Friends who are kind to one another at one moment often become exceedingly cruel the next. Most children accept such vacillation as a normal part of friendship. They expect that the damage done by cruelty will be quickly and easily repaired, which in fact is usually the case (Damon, 1988).

Although ups and downs are a normal part of childhood friendships, persistent rejection or extreme cruelty is not. In fact, peer rejection is one of the best predictors of psychosocial problems in later life. In a classic study, Cowen, Pederson, Babigian, Izzo, and Trost (1973) examined which of many psychological assessments in third grade was the best predictor of later psychiatric problems. Negative peer evaluations, based on classmates' nominations for negative roles in a class play, were better predictors than clinical impressions, academic achievement measures, or teacher ratings. Notably, however, self-ratings also had predictive significance.

Rejected children are generally known to lack social traits and skills needed to get along with others. They often do not know how to gain entry into peer groups. Instead of finding a cooperative role as their peers play, rejected children are more likely to bring negative attention to themselves by either too boldly intruding (disagreeing or commenting about themselves) or by too meekly hanging around without joining in (Putallaz & Gottman, 1981).

Besides having difficulty gaining entry, rejected children are not very good at being friends. Rather than being attentive, helpful, approving, and cooperative, rejected children are more often self-absorbed, uncooperative, disruptive, and inappropriately hostile (Hartup, 1984; Rubin, 1980).

Peer rejection is thus in large measure caused by behavioral problems, particularly those associated with hyperactivity and conduct disorders. Nonetheless, these behavior problems are aggravated and perpetuated by children's own developing beliefs and attitudes. Rejected children may develop negative reputations that are hard to shake off, despite their best efforts to change. Rejected children are also likely to develop negative attitudes both toward themselves and others (the proverbial chip on the shoulder). They may come to see rejection as a permanent reflection of their own inadequacies rather than as a temporary social problem to be solved. These negative attitudes in turn lead rejected children toward further negative social experiences. Hostile, rejected children may join with other such children in deviant peer groups (Patterson, DeBarsyshe, & Ramsey, 1989). Victimized children may come to accept their negative identity, inviting further victimization (Rothbaum & Weisz, 1989).

Negative attitudes perpetuate negative behaviors. Avoiding or breaking such negative cycles requires the adults' attention to changing attitudes and behaviors. Considerable progress has been made by having adults help children acquire better social skills, particularly through the use of modeling and role play techniques (Asher & Renshaw, 1981). But attention must also be paid to changing negative reputations, identities, and social dynamics. In some cases, this may require directly confronting children with the problem. One first grade teacher we know asked her students to agree to ignore the attention-seeking noises of a disruptive child. Imagine the sense of power and good will these children experienced when they successfully managed this social problem.

Of course, children not only reject others with poor social skills, they also tend to reject children on more trivial grounds. Stereotypes and rigid conventions abound in middle childhood. Boys who are labeled sissies and girls who are deemed ugly, for example, are susceptible to attack. Strikingly, Harter (1990) finds that children's feelings about their physical appearance is a central component in global self-esteem in the later elementary years.

Although persistent social rejection undoubtedly poses a serious risk to self-esteem, it is important to recognize that in most cases popularity is not highly related to self-esteem (Hartup, 1984 p. 246). Children do not have to be highly popular to feel good about themselves, any more than they have to feel exceptionally good about themselves to be accepted. In fact, there is some evidence that children with moderate levels of self-esteem are better accepted than children who express either high or low self-esteem (Hartup, 1984).

As in other areas of developing competence, we suspect that children do best when their attention can be focused on the tasks at hand, namely making and repairing friendships, and entering and cooperating in peer groups. Children who are self-preoccupied, either with a sense of inferiority or superiority, are unlikely to exhibit the attention, empathy, and helpfulness so necessary for social relationships.

All children need to find positive social niches in the classroom, with no child being repeatedly rejected, but it is not necessary to encourage all children to be popular, outgoing, and friendly. It is important, for example, not to confuse shyness with low self-esteem. Some children are naturally slow to warm up socially and this has little to do with their general feelings of competence. Respect should be given to a wide range of individual differences in patterns of friendship and sociability.

Virtue, moral worth

Just as school-age children are coming to evaluate themselves according to new standards of competence, power, and acceptance, so they are evaluating themselves according to new standards of virtue. Kohlberg (1976) described this period as one of conventional morality. Children typically evaluate themselves in terms of publicly shared norms of behavior.

Being *good* or *nice* in middle childhood means two things. First, to be good in the classroom means to be well-behaved, hard working, and respectful of authority. *Bad* or *mean* children are disobedient, disruptive, and lazy. Teachers naturally insist on these values in their efforts to manage children and socialize them into the student role (Covington, 1989). Second, to be a *nice* friend or classmate means to be cooperative, helpful, and attentive.

As we saw in the previous section, children who upset the teachers are often the same children who are rejected by peers. Children who are hostile and lack self-control often fail to meet teacher standards of good behavior as well as peer standards of friendship. Although these patterns begin in preschool, they are aggravated in middle childhood as children experience more demanding conventions of appropriate behavior. Reputations and identities — good/nice or bad/mean — may become crystallized as children increasingly view themselves and others in terms of enduring psychological traits.

Fairness is an important factor in children's developing understanding and appreciation of values underlying authority and friendship.

The dominant moral standard of middle childhood is *be fair,* the critical refrain being "It's not fair!" (Damon, 1988). Children at this age are constantly demanding and debating fairness. Although this marks an important advance in children's social and moral understanding, children's initial notions of fairness are initially quite naive. Fairness is often equated with sameness or equality (Damon, 1988). Children can be sticklers for insisting that things be literally equal and the same, a standard that helps explain the sometimes rigid conformity and conventionality of middle childhood.

Fairness is an important factor in children's developing understanding and appreciation of values underlying authority and friendship. Whereas preschool children view authority as simply a matter of power, school-age children learn to better appreciate and question the legitimacy of authority. In this light, children come to see obedience less as a matter of force and will, and more as a matter of respect.

Such respect includes a new sense of fairness in terms of the principle of reciprocity: Children recognize that they should be helpful and obedient toward adults who are helpful and nurturant toward them (Damon, 1988). As a consequence, children may be incensed by a child who treats a nice teacher unfairly, just as they condone disobedience against a teacher who is mean (If she's not nice to me, I don't have to be nice to her).

Peer relations are also increasingly guided by fairness according to the principle of reciprocity: If I help you, you will help me; if I'm nice to you, you'll be nice to me. This new standard both encourages greater cooperation and may explain the derision of children who fail to meet the standard.

Combined with new standards, there is a new sense of responsibility in middle childhood. Children are increasingly expected to be responsible for their own behavior, whether this be finishing their work or cooperating with peers. Along with responsibility comes a sense of guilt. For the most part, guilt is a healthy emotion (Damon, 1988; Fraiberg, 1959). As Damon (1988) carefully points out, based on a study by Miller and Swanson of school children's expressions of guilt, "the flagship form [of guilt] was an adaptive orientation towards self-criticism in service of the self's optimal relations with others" (p. 24).

An important goal of middle childhood is to foster *constructive* self-criticism and guilt, while avoiding debilitating anxiety and self-condemnation. In fact, young children initially have difficulty accepting criticism (Stipek & Mac Iver, 1989). They rarely offer self-criticism, and often defend against criticism from others. One likely reason is that lacking a differentiated understanding of their traits and abilities, they tend to interpret criticism globally and personally; the absence of a star on a paper may elicit a barrage of negative inferences: "The teacher hates me, I hate the teacher, I'm stupid, the teacher's stupid." It takes time and support and clarification for children to differentiate the implications of criticism and take it constructively.

Guilt appears to be a more constructive emotion than shame. Guilt arises when children see their unacceptable behavior as a failure of effort and responsibility. Guilt prompts efforts toward improvement and restitution. Shame arises when children see unacceptable behavior as a result of some personal inadequacy that may defeat further efforts toward change (Covington, 1989).

The meshing of the developmental needs and capacities of young school-age children with the expectations of the major institution in their lives, the school, offers a daunting challenge to those who wish to nourish a healthy sense of self-esteem in children. The research evidence points to the complicated picture of the interplay between children's developing beliefs and behaviors in the context of their changing social experiences. Chapter 6 will consider ways in which we can apply what we are learning about acceptance, power, competence, and moral virtue in order to influence healthy development in these aspects of self-esteem.

Part II

Beyond self-esteem: Implications for practitioners

Introduction

How do adults promote self-esteem?

CHILDREN'S FEELINGS ABOUT LOVE AND POWER, virtue and eagerness to please, competence and confidence, do not emerge in a vacuum, nor do they suddenly appear at a specific age. Rather, children gradually develop and learn—through experience, through language, through thoughtful adults, and through each other—who they are and what they can become.

Recent books and articles on developmentally appropriate practice all recognize that the adult is crucial (Bailey & Barton, 1982; Bredekamp, 1987; Godwin & Schrag, 1988; Muzick & Householder, 1986). But gone from them is the picture of the didactic teacher that many of us knew. In its place is an image of the adult who cares about young children as mediator, facilitator, collaborator, and engager.

The practices recommended here are the foundations for positive development of very young children in the family, in family day care, in hospitals, in child care programs, in elementary schools, and in all other settings where young children spend their days (and occasionally nights as well).

The review of the literature in Part I has important implications for guiding practices in early childhood education. What excellent teachers have known through clinical practice and theory now has solid research support. Some of this research has been derived from studies of good parenting, but our primary purpose is to address this section to caregivers, early childhood educators, and teacher educators. The following basic principles are abstracted from the evidence presented in Part I.

Adult feedback must be authentic

So many of us naively believe, as did one of our student/practitioners, that "You can never give a child enough praise or positive reinforcement.

91

If children hear these kinds of things repeatedly while growing up, it will help them have more confidence and self-esteem as adults."

Such an approach to parenting and teaching ignores the evidence, including that which we reviewed in Chapters 1 through 3. It even ignores personal experience which, if reviewed objectively and in depth, tells us otherwise. Indeed, heavy doses of well-intended but often empty praise, taken as a cure-all for low self-esteem, can be counterproductive (see Cannella, 1986, for a review of the research). Children need coaches — adults who realize the full implications of their efforts on the child's developing sense of self and act accordingly — rather than cheerleaders.

Praise, well-intentioned as it might be in the name of boosting self-esteem, can easily be overdone at any age. All too often, we unwittingly teach children to rely on the judgments of others rather than on their own evaluations based on experience. We say, "Good job!" or "That's right!" or award a sticker. Over and over.

We can better facilitate children's developing sense of themselves as valuable people through encouragement with more reasoned comments and efforts (Hitz & Driscoll, 1988). Consider how what you say about children's true accomplishments really affects their feelings of being loved, trusting and trusted, empowered, virtuous, and competent, and encourages them to tackle more challenges: "You got the ring to fit on the spindle all by yourself!" "Your puzzle took real persistence to finish."

Parent love is different from caregiver love, and so it should be. But all of us must be invested enough in the children we care about so we can provide the "affect attunement" Stern (1985) describes for infants and toddlers, but which continues to be necessary as children grow older. The importance of recognizing and labeling children's feelings and perceptions authentically was highlighted in Part I.

Fraiberg (1959) pointed out the very real harm intelligent, well-intentioned parents can inflict by trying to avert a child's experiencing anxiety. She described Doug, a 6-year-old who appeared to be an outgoing, happy-go-lucky child during the day but who suffered terrifying nightmares and wet the bed every night. He denied ever fearing anything and had a finely tuned ability to deny unpleasant topics (trips to the dentist or to the hospital) by referring to the delightful treats in store around these events. Fraiberg learned from his parents about their mode of dealing with Doug's anxiety from infancy. "Even when he was a baby they found themselves very upset by any of the usual manifestations of distress or pain. Their impulse at such times was to step in quickly and offer a distraction or an amusement or something that would provide immediate solace. 'Don't cry, dear. Look, baby, see the pretty bird!' " (pp. 276–277).

Fraiberg pointed out that Doug lacked anticipatory anxiety, so that unmodulated anxiety haunted him at night. All children need to learn to develop this anticipatory anxiety in order to design coping strategies to deal with even the everyday stresses of living. Tronick (1989) supports this with his concepts of interactive errors and repairs as described in Chapter 1.

Adults and children need goodness of fit

At the heart of our coaching skills is finding a goodness of fit between adults and children. A teacher's ability to work well with a particular age group may well be related to an ability to personally identify with the children's developmental needs and strivings (Rosen, 1972). Thus, parents or caregivers may enjoy working with dependent infants, but feel put off by children who can do it by themselves. Others may enjoy the spunky toddler years, and have no tolerance for the 24-hour dependency left behind in infancy. Some adults relish the inquiring minds of the "Why?" preschoolers, and feel relieved that the sometimes difficult twos have been replaced by eagerness to please. Yet others of us are thrilled with elementary-age children, who are independently reaching for increasingly abstract ideas.

Parents make a lifetime commitment to their children, so flexibility in meeting each day's variations in development is a must. Teachers and other caregivers have the option of devoting their professional lives to their most satisfying level(s) of development.

Scaffolding supports autonomy

The metaphor of "scaffolding" (Wood, Bruner, & Ross, 1976) is useful in understanding this process. This concept, derived from Vygotsky (1978) emphasizes that adults ideally gauge the amount of support and challenge necessary for optimal growth. Adults take the initiative in supplying supports when children are younger and gradually decrease these sorts of support to allow children to become more autonomous. In turn, the new autonomy brings with it new expectations and challenges, needing new forms of scaffolding.

Psychoanalytic writers (e.g., Mack, 1985) have expressed a similar idea in the notion of "optimal ego frustration." The goal is to ensure that children are optimally challenged, so that they experience both the limits of their abilities, as well as the success of overcoming these limits.

Individuals are different

Each child is different. Although we viewed children's development in the traditional ages and stages approach, individual temperaments differ (Chess & Thomas, 1987). Some children are person-oriented, while others are object-oriented (Abrams & Neubauer, 1976; Jennings, 1975). Some are patterners or dramatists (Shotwell, Wolf, & Gardner, 1979; Wolf & Gardner, 1978).

Further, children differ according to their families' cultures. In a recent article reviewing the family ecologies of ethnic minority children, the authors (Harrison, Wilson, Pine, Chan, & Buriel, 1990, p. 357) discuss adaptive strategies of minority families (African American, Native American/Alaskan Native, Asian Pacific American, and Hispanic) that are responses to ecological challenges: family extendedness ("a problem-solving and stress coping system" [p. 351]), role flexibility (sharing of parenting and breadwinning), biculturalism (that fosters more cognitive flexibility), and ancestral worldview ("collectivism or loyalty to the group in some form" [p. 354]).

Self-esteem is multifaceted

By now it should be clear that self-esteem is not a unitary, global construct. Acceptance, power and control, competence, and moral virtue are aspects of self-evaluation and are a part of character development.

Many parents and teachers seem frightened of setting limits for children, as if they will frustrate them and create a bundle of neuroses. Permissiveness can be as noxious as authoritarianism. We have been oversold on letting children act out aggressive impulses in a distortion of Freudian principles (Fraiberg, 1959); channeling those impulses begins in infancy. There are data to show that hostile aggression does not just go away and in fact escalates and causes children to be avoided and disliked (Coie & Dodge, 1988). Moral education has been neglected, and should have a place in an early childhood curriculum.

Children are resilient

As Fraiberg (1959) so wisely said:

> If we read our evidence correctly, it appears that parents [and caregivers] need not be paragons; they may be inexperienced, they may be permitted to err in the fashion of the species, to employ sometimes a wrong method or an unendorsed technique, and still have an excellent chance of rearing a healthy child if the bonds between parent and child are strong and provide the incentives for growth and development in the child. For the decisive

factors in mental health are the capacity for dealing with conflict, the ability to tolerate frustration, to adapt, and to find solutions that bring harmony between inner needs and outer reality. These qualities of the ego are themselves the product of the child's bonds to his parents, the product of the humanizing process. (pp. 301–302)

So — how can we implement these principles? The following chapters will describe how teachers and other caregivers can support, guide, encourage, and challenge children to become engaged in valued pursuits, thereby experiencing themselves in valued ways.

Chapter 4

Infancy and toddlerhood: Caring for children who are developing and consolidating a sense of self

A S WE HAVE SEEN, INFANTS ARE LEARNING TO TRUST OTHERS AND THEM-
SELVES, to feel lovable, loving, and competent, and to begin to realize their growing control over themselves and the world around them. These developments are the result of partnerships between the developing child and caring adults. At birth, the expectancies, personalities, and skills that parents bring to childrearing interact with the individual characteristics of the newborn. So begins a lifelong process of adaptation.

A key issue is how the infant is valued. Caregivers who value the newborn individual, regardless of its characteristics, seek to provide the support and scaffolding that best fits the infant's needs. Through such support, the infant not only comes to feel loved and secure, competent and powerful, but also develops genuine skills in self-regulation. This chapter makes recommendations to foster such positive beginnings.

Early infancy

Hospitals can be inhospitable places for new lives to make their appearance, and if the infant must be in the neonatal intensive care unit, the environment of necessity must be even more inhospitable (Freud, 1989a). For parents whose children need special medical attention, there may be a flurry of activity in learning more about the child's condition, prognosis, and caregiving requirements, and little time for getting to know their baby. From the first exchange of gazes in the delivery room, until the parents carefully place their child into an infant safety seat for the ride home, parents are setting in place patterns of interaction with their newborn. Eagerness to learn more about babies, and about this baby in particular, is usually at its height during this transitional period for adults and children (Klaus & Kennell, 1976).

Each baby has a unique temperament: "What an easy baby." "If only my baby could sleep for more than 3 hours at a time." Although some differences may be intensified, modified, or even reversed in part by caregiver responses, other differences appear to remain fairly stable. Shyness, even in very young babies, is one of those lingering personality traits (Kagan, Reznick, & Gibbons, 1989). Shy babies are highly reactive to their environment and tend to become disorganized by too much stimulation. Adults may need to buffer the noise, light, and people in shy babies' surroundings.

We have seen that newborns are already attuned to people within their environment, and especially are attracted to the human face (Spitz, 1965). Finding the just-right dosage (Tolpin, 1971) of evoking and responding to the baby's cues is a primary task for parents and caregivers of young babies. Most babies will look away when they've had enough. Others may begin to wail, or fall asleep. When babies are eager for more, they gaze back, and may thrash their arms and legs in excitement (Brazelton & Als, 1979; Stern, 1974).

Help the baby establish regularity

Predictability — physical and emotional — makes it possible for newborns to begin to regulate their own behaviors (Brazelton & Als, 1979). It also provides the foundation for trust and gives the baby the message that "You are worth caring for and loving."

Not so long ago, parents and medical care providers believed that babies should eat on a regular 4-hour schedule, and that loud, prolonged crying was "good for the lungs." Not so. We have seen that responding soon and sensitively to a crying newborn lessens the crying later in the first year. The baby has learned to count on help to come. Many babies get hungry much sooner than every 4 hours. Flexibility is important as we adjust our expectations to baby's cues about what is right and best for her or him.

But babies also need to find landmarks during caregiving that help to establish regularity. Everyday routines become predictable. During the routines, describe what you are doing, and tell baby what's coming up next. "There, the last snap is together. Now, up you come. Let's go fold the laundry." Authentically positive feedback — both personal and in the environment — helps infants and toddlers feel loved, effective, and eager to master both their internal and external worlds.

Offer security and comfort

Warmth and gentleness — in touch and tone of voice — seem like such common sense, but a reminder about this is important, especially for parents whose lives may be filled with an extra amount of stress (and lack of sleep) during the next few weeks. Both baby and caregiver benefit from quiet, relaxing feeding times, whether from breast or bottle. Play with baby by echoing sounds. Mirror baby's facial expressions. Comment on baby's state: You whisper, "My, aren't you a sleepy baby," or, as the sucking slows, comment, "It looks like you've had enough to drink for now." It's a time of special closeness, and should never be replaced by propping baby and bottle in a corner so you can get on with other tasks.

Other ways adults can appropriately establish the groundwork for promoting baby's self-esteem and beyond:

- Tune into baby's signals and respond appropriately. Look into the baby's eyes with affection and interest, letting baby be the guide for how much and how often. Respond to cries by meeting baby's needs.
- Establish trust and lovability. Cuddle baby tenderly during feeding, when reciting poetry or telling stories, when rocking in your favorite chair. Talk with baby about what is happening. Play together, especially during routines such as diapering and bathing.

4 to 9 months

This is often the period in which babies may enter group care. Caregivers need to know that babies at this age already exhibit early signs of real differentiation and a sense of themselves. They learn to sit by themselves, use their hands and mouths to explore everything, react to themselves in a mirror, and perhaps crawl. These milestones emerge when children feel loved and secure enough to reach out to the rest of the world.

Play games

Age-old games such as "Peek-A-Boo," "This Little Piggy," and "Where's Baby's Nose?" are ideal for babies who are beginning to distinguish themselves from others. All help baby establish "This is you" and "This is something else." Word games can be played during a bath, or when changing a diaper. Make the most of the hours spent in carrying out routines by creating playful games with words, music, and touch.

More intensely physical play, such as swinging or tossing the baby in the air, or helping baby to spring and jump, prepare leg muscles for walking (White, 1985). Most babies delight in the excitement, but watch for signals that say, "I've had enough" and then stop immediately and acknowledge baby's feelings. "You look like this isn't fun anymore. Let's do something quieter for a bit."

Authentically positive feedback helps infants and toddlers feel loved, effective, and eager to master their world.

Comments such as these are known as alter-ego talk (Schachter, 1979). Most parents and caregivers do it naturally. Stern (1985) has analyzed how these conversations help to highlight the child's core sense of self:

- Agency: "How high you can bounce!"
- History: "You want another little cuddle after I burp you, like we did at your last feeding?"
- Coherence: "You spotted me! This *is* mommy in the picture."
- Affectivity: "Watching that other baby really excites you!"

Embedded in all this play is our attitude about the baby as an individual and about the environment. Adults who take pleasure in playing with babies communicate that babies are important. Young infants are likely to mirror our feelings (Tronick, Cohn, & Shea, 1984). There's no way to tell a baby you're having a hard day that has nothing to do with them. As they grow older, they begin to interpret these feelings subjectively. Even as adults, we tend to blame ourselves when those close to us are moody or grumpy.

Explore things

Interest in toys also begins to flower through interchanges between adults and babies. The child's ability to grasp objects coincides with this development, and thus Brazelton and Als (1979) concluded that object play, which emerges at about 4 months, is the first true test of attachment.

Children need bright, clean, safe toys to practice their grasp, to discover the "pleasures in being the cause," the forerunner of a sense of efficacy (White, 1963), and to share with beloved others. But, they also need to be protected from the overstimulation of too many toys, especially if these toys are used to divert the babies from the more important relationships with people. Some guidelines for toys and play are:

- Offer toys that are just within, and outside, reach of babies who can now sit and are beginning to crawl. This strategy is an example of *scaffolding,* a challenge to the child's potential for new growth. On the floor or in a lap, babies love to smell, feel, and taste the bright, clean objects you offer. Talk about each toy with delight, rather than dumping a pile and leaving babies to their own devices. Describe the color, the texture, and the use for toys.
- Display an attitude about the environment that nourishes children's curiosity and sense of wonder about themselves and objects. Consider, for instance, a baby sitting on a blanket in the shade outdoors. A small hand reaches for the ant crawling by. What different messages can be conveyed about self and science: "Yuk, that's dirty," and you brush away the ant; or "Hey, look at that busy ant. It's carrying food back to its

family. Let's watch where it goes." Think about what you are saying, and how it affects baby's feelings about exploration.

- Select toys that can be grasped in small hands, yet are not so small that they present a choking hazard. When choosing toys, think about what the BABY can DO with the toy.

- Offer baby safe toys that encourage the child's active sensorimotor exploration: toys that make noise when they are batted at or shaken, teething toys, measuring spoons, a small unbreakable mirror, books made to be chewed, and sock puppets. Notice that most of these can be handmade or are just everyday household items. Expense is no clue to play value.

- Present a variety in texture — to touch and taste — that enables babies to learn in the ways they use best. Hard and smooth wood, shiny metal, rough and patterned fabric, and squeezy bright plastics all have their place.

- Display toys so babies can make a choice, thus enabling their competence. Low, open shelves are far better than a toy box or laundry basket into which everything is tossed. Spread books open on the floor. Note: Some of the best toys at this age are household items: pots and pans, old magazines, plastic containers, and clothespins.

Toys should not be provided at the expense of human interactions, however. Too many toys can make choices difficult, and may detract from the important work of getting to know other babies or adults. Offer just one or two items until you get the message that something else would be more fun. Through playful interactions with people and toys, babies build on the love and trust they have experienced to increasingly make things happen.

9 to 15 months

How heady it is for children at this age, who, thanks to their mobility, can control separations and reunions, thus demonstrating two salient developmental aspects of this period of separation-individuation.

Fine tune relationships

Play and caregiving routines remain the focus of daily life for infants and adults, whether at home or in child care programs.

Children now have the capacity to understand adult responses to their behaviors and to modify their reactions, as we saw with the children who would not crawl over the visual cliff (Sorce et al., 1985). Standing at the edge of the foam climbing cushions, arms outstretched, says "You can't

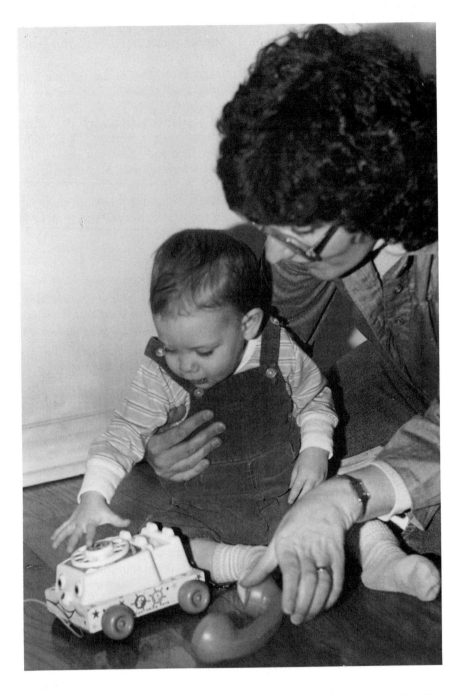

Adults who take pleasure in playing with babies communicate that babies are important.

do this by yourself, so I will catch you when you fall." Sitting nearby, watching, and informally commenting on the child's bravery in the precarious climb communicates trust that the child can do it alone. Many caregivers seem to have an exaggerated fear of danger and can convey this to babies to the detriment of their venturing into the world with confidence.

Through informed observation and empathy, caregivers also must constantly be alert to read the baby's intentions and feelings. We validate the baby's responses when we imitate, mirror, or label accurately the child's experiences (Stern, 1985). "The bunny pictures in that book are so funny! You're giggling and giggling."

Such strategies, coupled with a developmentally appropriate environment, solidify children's internal pictures of themselves and thus promote optimal growth of self-understanding and self-valuing.

Create a manageable environment

The tender, loving care that has characterized life so far will most likely be evidenced as children take increasing control over their environment and demonstrate empathy for others. They can plan actions, know what to expect in many situations, and rely on rituals. Children by age one are increasingly in charge of what happens to them. Adults can facilitate the process toward independence in a variety of ways.

Attachment has occurred and separation reactions often surface during this period. Caregivers might enlist children's assistance in comforting a child who is having a difficult time saying good-bye for the day. "Let's all go to the window and wave to Josemar's daddy. See you this afternoon, Dad!" Posting family photographs at children's eye level, making recordings of family members singing a favorite song, and allowing children to bring their blankets with them all can help children better manage their strong feelings of attachment and their distress during separation (Ayers, 1989).

Games and pretend play are other ways that young walkers demonstrate their dawning self-awareness. A modified version of "Simon Says" gives children an opportunity to show their understanding of self and others. "Simon Says touch your toes." "Simon Says hold a friend's hand."

Simple props for pretend play — trucks, pots and pans, shoes, dolls — enable children to play out their emerging understanding of the roles of others in relation to themselves. Other toys that invite action, such as containers to nest, magazines to tear, wooden blocks to stack, objects to float, and balls to roll, are a good match for children who are learning the power that arises from what they do.

The importance of monitoring the amount of stimulation children can handle was dramatically demonstrated by Collard (1979). An initial comparison of institutionalized and home-reared children indicated that those in the institution showed "significantly less exploration and fewer schemas to the toys" (p. 58). In response, the institution's supervisor added a profusion of toys and placed the infants in groups of 10 or more for most of the day, with these results:

Instead of looking happier than the infants I had studied there earlier, they appeared to be stressed by overstimulation. Their exploration had a frantic quality to it: their attention span with toys was very short; they seldom smiled and often fussed or cried. Some of the babies withdrew completely by crawling under a crib and going to sleep on the floor. (p. 59)

This knowledge raises the issue of how many toys and how many children are enough. It is unreasonable to expect children to share spontaneously until they are well into the preschool years. Too many children in a group can be overwhelming. Even when small groups of very young children play together, it is wise to have more than one of the most favorite toys. Otherwise, snatching and hoarding are inevitable, and grabbing, hitting, and even biting may be promoted. Worse yet, those who are uninformed may be tempted to label the more aggressive children as "bad" and those who are docile as "good." Such epithets can easily become self-fulfilling prophecies.

We can see, then, that small groups of infants, guided by a kind and generous caregiver who can accord children the power of initiating and engaging in delightful play, makes for a predictable and challenging environment. Such an atmosphere of support and sensitivity sets the stage for impending toddlerhood.

15 to 24 months

The cognitive, motor, and affective leaps in development that take place during this year lead to ever greater self-awareness, but also some stormy times. As children rush toward independence, they can also cognitively realize the impact of separation. They may dig in their heels, establishing their autonomy through occasional power assertions, better known as "NO!" Depending upon the adult's own struggles with autonomy and control, toddlers can anger, disappoint, or delight caregivers (Mahler, Pine, & Bergman, 1975) as they alternately cling and then refuse. Children may also be shaken by their inability to separate as easily as before.

The caregiver's view of the child is the crux of this struggle between autonomy versus shame and doubt, as so vividly described by Erikson (1950). Adult reactions to this normal developmental process can range from "Don't be a crybaby. You're a big boy now" and "How dare you contradict me" to "You really wish you could go to work with Mom.

An understanding and knowledgeable caregiver can help children feel comfortable with, and in control of, their growing autonomy.

Would you like to call her after snack?" and "You can choose. Would you like a pear or an orange?"

As we have seen, labels repeatedly assigned to a child such as stubborn, sassy, or naughty tend to live with the child as self-fulfilling prophecies. Words can and do hurt. Normally spunky toddlers, when confronted with scornful treatment such as these labels, generally take one of three paths. They can become oppositional, retreat to passive-aggressive dawdling, or languish as shy, withdrawn, and defeated.

On the other hand, an understanding and knowledgeable caregiver can help children feel comfortable with, and in control of, their growing autonomy. Language is the powerful vehicle through which we can promote children's positive feelings about themselves.

Support independence

Toddlers who feel they have some control over their lives are less likely to feel the need to resist adults. Therefore, activities and the environment should be structured to enable toddlers to be as self-directed and independent as possible. That means small groups, hands-on projects, and child-centered activities.

Strategies to engage and challenge children include the provision of toys, activities, an appropriate environment, and separations that are eased by routines.

Toys. Select toys that present problems for children to solve: puzzles, blocks, pounding benches, kitchen utensils, sorting boxes, large beads to string, clay, telephones, shopping carts, books with short stories.

Activities. Toddlers are exceedingly curious. Short walks around the neighborhood can reveal many wonders, from construction in progress to the sound of a motorcycle passing by. They love to be part of the action and enjoy brief finger plays and action songs. "The Wheels on the Bus" is always a big hit, but try to vary the children's repertoire beyond "Open Them/Shut Them," the Alma Mater of innumerable preschools! Water play is so absorbing. Choose activities that toddlers shape as they DO.

Environment. Store toys on low, open shelves where children can locate and return their choices. Toddler clothes should promote independence, especially as they become more interested in learning to use the toilet. Zippers, elastic, large snaps, and Velcro are far easier to master than buttons and buckles. Mirrors have many functions, and are not just a token gesture toward enhancing self-esteem (Greenberg, 1988).

Give children two good choices whenever possible, so they feel in control and at the same time learn from the consequences of their own actions. Power struggles are averted when children choose. "Do you want your teddy on your cot, or on the chair by your cot, while you nap?" "Would you like a shower or a bath?" as opposed to statements that children ignore such as "Are you ready for your nap/bath now?" or "It's nap/bath time. Get in here." Throughout the early childhood years, as children grow more adept at decision making, offer a broader range of choices to increasingly scaffold children's skills in this area.

Separations. Caregivers and parents must work together to establish routines that make separations less traumatic for all involved. Some parents spend a minute or two on arrival in child care, for example, helping the child get settled. "Your lunch goes here in your cubby. There's a note inside for Darrell to read to you before you eat. Now, where would you like to start this morning?" Others leave a beloved object for the child, such as a scarf, as a reminder of their love. Here's an example of a family day care mother helping a 2-year-old settle in.

> Just as Gina joins the cooking crew, Carol arrives. She comes only two mornings a week, and she is not really settled in on this day when her mother hurries off. Chana holds her and rocks her but she sobs and sobs. "I want Mommy." Soon her face is puffy and red and dripping. Chana, wiping nose and eyes, rocks her and softly chants a kind of soothing mantra: "Mommies go away and mommies come back; mommies go away and mommies come back." (Ayers, 1989, pp. 44–45)

Family pictures, recordings of parents telling a favorite story, and one's security blanket continue to help children restore their equilibrium while acknowledging how difficult growing up and away can be.

Talk with, not at, toddlers

In toddlerhood, the child tests her or his power, sometimes contrary to the wishes of powerful, beloved, and/or feared adults. Parents and teachers alike must prepare themselves to support children through this feisty period. The match between caregiver and child is especially important. A toddler program is no place for teachers who feel threatened by power struggles and children's assertions of independence!

Fortunately, there are developmentally appropriate ways to talk with toddlers that are "designed to foster the motivation for active learning in children, to enhance their self-confidence, their sense of power, and their feelings of mastery over the environment" (Schachter, 1979, p. 163). These also happen to be the attributes of self-evaluation. Research on Schachter's Talking with Young Children (TYCH) curriculum has led to development of the following strategies (Schachter & Strage, 1982, p. 90) that underscore other developmental teaching techniques as well (Blank, Rose, & Berlin, 1978):

- Attract and maintain the child's attention. Address a question to the child, use a higher pitched voice, or talk in a whisper. "Who can carry this bucket?"
- Simplify speech. Most of us do this naturally as we take care to model sounds, meanings, grammar, and conversational patterns. On the other hand, baby talk is never appropriate. "Your sandwich is falling apart. Let's put the meat back inside."
- Repeat and rephrase our own speech. Again, "This process is so 'natural'—that speakers are only barely aware of using it" (Ferguson, 1977, p. 223). "It's time to put the markers away. Please put the lids on the markers before they go in the box."
- Repeat and rephrase the child's speech. Extend what the child says. "Ball." "Whew, look at your ball rolling. It's going so fast!"
- Map words onto the child's experiences. Speak in the present, and describe the child's desires or activities. "The sand is falling through the holes in the sieve. See how softly it falls into your dish."
- Speak for the child, as when adults assume the child's role in the conversation. "Your face tells me you'd rather not taste these crackers."
- Speak responsively with the child. Follow the child's lead in conversation. "Fishing." "Did you go fishing with Grandma last night? Tell me what happened."

Even rules for behavior can be stated in positive terms, so children know what TO DO, rather than only what to avoid: We walk indoors. Spills get wiped up with our sponge. We use our words to solve problems. An occasional "No" is necessary for safety's sake, of course, and will not cramp a toddler's style, if used judiciously.

Working with and parenting toddlers requires a great deal of patience and forethought. But when adults take into consideration the four critical dimensions of self-evaluation and the developmental process in general, we can make the best of even the most trying times.

2 to 3 years

During the course of this year, children's language flowers, and with it the ability to engage in social relationships and dramatic play more fully than before. Children consolidate their gains, more clearly establish where they fit into the scheme of things, and solidify their sense of self. Adults remain at the forefront in facilitating growth during this period when power struggles gradually lessen and children strive to be fair and honest.

Be authentic

Between the second and third birthdays, children can begin to view themselves more broadly. Rather than labeling and demeaning children, we need to find adjectives that communicate respect, even when setting limits or mediating disputes.

Consider all the messages in statements such as "What a bad boy you were to grab the book," or "You're too selfish. Why can't you share?" Instead, responses such as "You were angry when you grabbed the book. What words could you use to tell Selia you would like the book back?" or "How generous of you to share your crackers with Molly" help children maintain their dignity while providing them with skills to resolve difficulties between each other without adult interference.

> Now the problems that young children face in social relationships are considerable. How to get others' attention and cooperation, how to cope with disagreements, how to understand another's intentions, how to provide comfort for another when in distress — how to manage their social world. A child's sense of self-efficacy is likely to come, then, in large part from solving these problems, from having control over such social matters. In being effective in these matters, a core of children's feelings about themselves is established. (Dunn, 1988a, p. 177)

Parents and teachers alike can model friendly interactions between each other, and with children. As observers, we can watch as two children resolve a disagreement themselves, or facilitate a discussion when emotions exceed the toddler vocabulary and self-control. We can encourage discussion: "Joey, Mike says he thought you were finished with the car. How can you tell him what you were doing?"

Generous. Kind. Strong. Cooperative. Persistent. Brave. These words, and other similarly descriptive positive adjectives, are the staples of good childrearing practice, but should be applied judiciously, to avoid comparisons to other children (e.g., "Look how cooperative Marcus is!" implies the rest of the children aren't).

Even adults relish being described with friendly adjectives. A well-to-do business owner visited a child care center as part of a grant-award program. As the group talked, the director mentioned the businessman's empathy. He delightfully burst out: "She called me empathetic!" Apparently he discovered an aspect of himself of which he had previously not been consciously aware.

So it is with children. Of course, we must take care to accurately reflect their actions and accompanying feelings. If we consistently attribute positive or negative motivations to them, regardless of their true motivations, they will likely misinterpret, mislabel, or lose touch with their true feelings. "You're doing a good job" has become a hackneyed phrase because it is doled out for even the most ordinary behaviors (Hitz & Driscoll, 1988).

Fair and honest appraisals of children's actions, feelings, and opinions can go far to help children evaluate themselves and to modify behaviors that are inappropriate. "It is really hard to wait to be picked up at night." "Sometimes new babies make us feel jealous. We wish Mom could spend more time with us, too." Frustration accompanies growth. Children mature when interactions with adults are candid and heartfelt.

Encouragement, rather than praise, is far more effective. Consider the different messages in this comparison of praise and encouragement.

Praise: "Ginny's the best cleanup person in the block area." (Hitz & Driscoll, 1988, p. 12).

Encouragement: "You picked up many more blocks than you have ever picked up before," or "When you help us pick up the blocks we all get finished much sooner" (p. 12).

Encourage growth through play

Two-year-olds, who are still working to resolve separation issues and understand object constancy, are intrigued with toys and games that involve appearances and disappearances. Huge cardboard boxes, Kitten-in-the-Kegs, Magic Slates, and puppet stages all contribute to children's sense of efficacy and control (Harter, 1983), a crucial aspect of self-evaluation (Dunn, 1988a). Small doses of being in control over separations and reappearances help children manage the strong feelings aroused by daily separations from beloved adults (Freud, 1965).

Imitative play is also becoming more prevalent during this period, so equipment should include toys that elicit representation, such as dolls, dress-up clothes, sturdy adult work tools, and housekeeping items. For generations, symbolic play has centered around daily events:

It is, of course, the familiarity of eating procedures to all of them that makes it possible for the actors in these scenes to understand each other, and that makes dinner play occur most frequently as the first form of group dramatics among 2-year-olds. Bedding play runs it a close second, for all know that lying down means "going to bed" or "sleeping." (Woodcock, 1941, p. 227)

Teachers and parents can model and facilitate playfulness, and then switch roles to become an appreciative audience. Recall this same 2-year-old may get confused by pretend play initiated by an adult. Props provide ideas, and thus should be varied to stimulate thinking about new themes: medical checkups, grocery store (complete with computer scanner, of course), and transportation are popular because of the shared context.

If children are having difficulty organizing play, tuned-in adults can offer suggestions or ask questions to help children get a sense of direction: "Let's see, if you're taking the bus to the beach, you'll need towels, swimsuits, and money for bus fare." Join in a bit, if necessary, to sustain the action. "I'll be the ice cream truck driver who visits the beach." Bow out as the children pick up on the cues for more involved play.

In just a few short years, infants and toddlers have consolidated their sense of self. They have begun to wrestle with issues that will confront them all their lives: trust, love, power, separation, self-evaluation, conflict resolution, imagination, learning, and a host of others. The fabric of human worth is woven (or unraveled) each day, as children move toward the new challenges of the preschool years.

Chapter 5

Preschool: Guiding children who are testing and evaluating the self

INFANTS AND TODDLERS WHO HAVE EXPERIENCED SECURE ATTACHMENTS and good scaffolding usually approach the new challenges of preschool years with a fair sense of confidence, initiative, and resilience. On the other hand, children who have experienced less supportive environments may need extra support to compensate both for their own negative internal working models and the lack of personal and social skills. In between these extremes, many children exhibit islands of confidence combined with areas of vulnerability. In any case, children's developing sense of self must be supported in the new arena of the preschool years. This section offers recommendations to teachers and parents on how to sensitively meet the individual needs of children during this period.

Adults coach young children

Gut-level ideas about how parents and teachers improve self-esteem are simply not enough. We have so much information about why certain practices are more effective than others that we cannot ignore the evidence. As children move into the preschool years, the effects of our interactions with them are already unfolding. We must intensify our efforts to act in ways that engage them and promote their competence.

Understand and accept yourself

Before we can guide children to know themselves, we must first understand and accept ourselves. We have seen that the most effective teachers are those who are well-matched with the age of the children.

The necessity for introspection and self-examination has been highlighted by Derman-Sparks and her colleagues (1989). Our attitudes about racism, sexism, and abilities are deeply ingrained from our own experiences, and can easily be passed on to children — to the detriment of their self-perceptions. Although Derman-Sparks addresses teachers, parents' goals for independent, competent children are similar:

> To enable every child: to construct a knowledgeable, confident self-iden-tity; to develop a comfortable, empathic, and just interaction with diversity; and to develop critical thinking and the skills for standing up for oneself and others in the face of injustice. (p. IX)

Note how these goals parallel Coopersmith's antecedents of self-esteem (attention, limits, and respect) and Baumrind's findings about authoritative parenting. Adults so unwittingly can perpetuate stereo-types and model destructive attitudes:

- We may permit boys to denigrate girls. "You're not strong! You don't even have muscles," said one 3-year-old boy to a female peer.
- We may overlook or even allow racial denigration. "You're dirty!"
- We may patronize a child with disabilities. "Remember, we always let Tony go first because he's slower."

Such incidents either reinforce what children already wrongly believe, or teach biases directly to children. By accepting such behavior (ours or the children's) we demonstrate lack of respect for the child to whom the biases are directed.

Children need the firm limits of adults to stop the stereotyping. Children need positive models of adults who show real acceptance and re-spect. Before we can do either, we must be aware of our own biases — about age, race, sex, ability, and any other human characteristics — and seek to grow in our respect for others.

Discipline wisely

Parents and teachers alike seem to dwell on children's behavior. Disci-pline books are best sellers. Teachers flock to workshops on classroom management. Yet the fine tuning necessary to provide the support and challenges applied in scaffolding means much more emphasis on self understanding and a depth of understanding of children as individuals with varying degrees of competence.

We have seen how children's behavior is closely linked to their per-ceptions of themselves, even as infants and toddlers. And we have seen how parenting styles affect children's self-esteem. Clarke-Stewart and Friedman (1987) conclude:

> The best discipline for parents who wish to foster their children's social, cognitive, and moral development seems to be to create an atmosphere of warm approval, praise, and acceptance, and then to explain why the child should act in particular ways and to intervene actively when the child acts otherwise — this kind of discipline appeals to children's pride, compe-tence, and concern for others. (p. 363)

How are these principles, which are equally applicable to teachers of preschool children, applied in everyday situations? We offer these two broad guidelines (see Honig, 1985).

1. Balance acceptance, firm limits, and respect for children. All of these actions lead to increased self-control and empathy for others, which in turn directly affect children's assessments of themselves.

Children's individuality—personality, family, culture, physical presence—must be appreciated in both conscious and unconscious ways. Using a child's primary language to communicate, for instance, reaffirms one of the cores of the child's identity.

Rules for children's behavior should continue to be stated in positive terms, and explained in ways that make them meaningful. A good rule might be "Sand is for digging." The reasons for the rule: Sand hurts our eyes. Sand is hard to get out of our hair. If sand gets in the grass, we won't have any more sand in which to play. Preschoolers are usually eager to help set up and follow classroom rules when they understand the purpose is to ensure that their day goes smoothly.

Hurting others should never be allowed, either by adults or other children. Nothing is so destructive of children's trust or attachment as an out-of-control person who lashes out at others with deeds or words. Angry feelings can be accepted, but channeled into pounding clay or using words to express feelings.

Setting rules is relatively easy. Enforcing them is not. But again we must rely on what we know about the effects of our actions and attitudes on children's behavior. We know that children who are subjected to harsh discipline (yelling, too many or unreasonable rules, excessive and/or physical punishment) are likely to become hostile and aggressive. Bribes (ice cream cones or smiley-face stickers, for example) can backfire in the long run. Such overdone praise destroys children's intrinsic motivation; children lose interest in doing anything just for the pleasure of doing it. Being inconsistent in enforcement or making empty threats only encourages children to continue to break rules, always hopeful that they won't get caught or punished this time.

If our goals are to help children respect self and others, they need to be helped to see how their behavior affects themselves and others. Simple explanations or thought-provoking questions, offered when children are calm enough to be receptive, are effective tools. A child who is losing friends because she is so bossy might be urged to see the effects of her behavior on other children: "When you tell Lizette what to do, does she decide to play with you for very long?" A child who is rapidly diminishing the art supply box might be encouraged to think through the implications of his behavior: "If you use up all the ribbons for pasting, what will happen when your friends come to paste?"

By modeling behavior we want children to imitate, we are preparing caring, responsible human beings to live in a civilized world.

The superhero play so dear to children's hearts and so troublesome to teachers has a place in the curriculum as Paley (1984) has clearly documented. Such play gives an opportunity to test power, control, competence, and even moral virtue. Pointing out the multi-faceted roles of such characters (e.g., "Yes, Batman does fly around with a cape, but he also lives in a Batcave. Why don't you build one here in the block corner?") helps keep the play going but in a constructive mode.

Even toddlers, with a little help from an adult, can begin to resolve disagreements among themselves by using words instead of fists. Preschoolers should be well on their way to working out fair solutions among themselves, rather than relying on adults to referee — thus robbing children of the opportunity to feel in control about what happens to them and to feel competent to deal with social situations.

When a child comes running to tattle, "Teacher . . ." the best response is to guide the child back to the other party, and expect the children to discuss what happened and to come up with some ideas about how to solve the problem. THEY agree on the situation, THEY figure out what to do about it, and THEY choose what happens next. Mastery and autonomy are developed here!

2. Supply authentic feedback. Children are eager to please parents and teachers, so they often call out "Look at me!" or "See what I did." Tailor your response to the situation and the child by using adjectives that describe some positive aspect of the child's effort or its elements, rather than the product (see Schirrmacher, 1986). "Look how you made your brush strokes go back and forth." "You walked so gracefully across the balance beam." Catch all children doing well — not just the stars or those who constantly seek reassurance.

Further, don't be afraid to give honest criticism. Parents and teachers seem frightened by the idea of giving children negative feedback as if such comments will cause neuroses. Adults need to let children know that they do not condone raw aggression, lying, stealing, or cruelty. As Fraiberg says,

> Of course, it would also be wrong to threaten a child, as parents did in other times, with police action, detention homes or hell-fire and cause a small culprit to feel he was a dangerous criminal. We can teach moral attitudes without resorting to such cruel methods. (p. 266)

By modeling behaviors we want children to imitate (e.g., *not* hurting children, and *not* lying ourselves) and by our reactions when children do such things, we are preparing caring, responsible human beings to live in a civilized world.

Children pick up on adult judgments and moral values. They are also keenly aware when adults favor the stereotypic "good girl" and who adults view as "bad." A friend, who was one of a pair of female fraternal twins, still recalls the pain and embarrassment she felt when people would approach them and comment to their mother, "This is the pretty one, so this one must be the smart one." Children also are quick to detect adult phoniness and meaningless praise (Damon, 1988). Not every child's drawing can be "Wonderful!" every time!

Negative affect can interfere with cognition and disrupt social relations (Collins & Gunnar, 1990). But negative self-experiences are not all ruinous, if children are helped to learn from their experiences and apply their learning to future events. "You're disappointed that the purple paint covered up your yellow flower. Dark colors usually hide lighter ones." Negative self-feelings can constructively motivate personal improvement, just as overly positive self-feelings can result in complacency.

When we think about the implications of our statements and actions, and proceed accordingly, we are far more likely to encourage development of all dimensions of children's self-esteem. Part of this responsibility lies in enabling children to develop social skills.

Foster children's friendships

Friends are increasingly the eyes through which children judge themselves. In fact, young children's friends often shape behavior more than parents or teachers.

Paley (1988) writes about 3-year-olds who repeatedly ask "Are you my friend?" She describes Christopher, whose behavior is at times distasteful to her, and how Mollie develops a friendship with him that accepts his off-the-wall conversations. Eventually, the friendship helps Christopher modify his behavior. Adults at times must allow children to work through their own challenges, even so early in their lives.

At 4, the lure of the group is even stronger. Children become quite exclusive in their attempts to define themselves as group members (Curry & Arnaud, 1984). In the thinking of a 4-year-old, you can only belong to a group if there's someone else who can't.

A gifted teacher describes her ideas about helping children deal with each other:

> They're intensely interested in groups, in their families, friends, strangers, other kids. And at a very young age kids begin to socialize, to be interested in themselves in relation to others, in group play. Of course, they're still self-centered, but they develop rapidly into an awareness of their own limits as well as their own rights. Three-year-olds have a pretty strong sense of what's fair and what's unfair, and that sense isn't always self-serving. (Ayers, 1989, p. 62)

Children are as eager to please each other as they are to please adults, sometimes even more so, as Paley (1988) again illustrates so well:

Trembling in anger, Christopher holds up a fistful of paper. "I got more than you. I can get any piece of paper because you're not the boss!" The boys glance furtively in my direction, wondering if the situation has deteriorated enough for me to interfere. The timing of my entrance is tricky, but tears usually work well with me. Today, however, Christopher keeps them from brimming over.

"What are you talkin' about? Mollie's never going to play with you. She's my friend. Mollie, Mollie. . . ."

"Are you playing with him or us?" Barney demands.

"Say us, say us," Frederick pleads.

Mollie purses her lips primly. "I'm still friends with the whole of everyone. Nighttime, nighttime, everyone goes to bed. The rainbow is outside the window."

Miraculously, the tension dissolves. Rainbow Brite has accomplished what a teacher seldom can, the resolution of a conflict without disturbing the rhythm of the play. The children know when the emergency is over before I do. (pp. 17–18)

This example in no way implies that adults should abdicate their roles and allow children to learn social skills as in *Lord of the Flies*. It is essential for parents and teachers alike to take these three steps.

1. Nourish the tendrils of friendship. Welcome new children, perhaps by asking another child to assist you as the newcomer's partner for the day. Encourage parents to support children's friendships with visits to each other's homes. Read a book about a shared interest with just two or three children on your lap. Notice activities that appeal to shy/withdrawn/disliked children and create situations to involve them with more popular children in a mutually satisfying activity (see Honig, 1987). Pairs or small group tasks that inspire cooperation are excellent friendship facilitators.

2. Help children learn social skills. Modeling, by adults and other children, may be all that is needed for children to become more socially adept. At times, it may be necessary to provide children with examples of words they might use to indicate their interest in joining a group at play or to resolve a conflict (Hazen & Black, 1989; Honig, 1987). A teacher, hand in hand with a shy child, might ask the ticket taker whether help was needed to carry luggage to the plane.

We also know that children tend to live up to our expectations for them, as so aptly illustrated by Bill, a very large 4-year-old bull-in-the-china-shop boy. His blundering into ongoing play caused him to be rejected over and over. "Get out of here," and "You can't play," were the daily responses to his overtures. His teachers noted that this rejection began upon his arrival, after other children had already begun to play. They made a special effort to greet him warmly, "Here comes Bill! Now we can really start our day!" The other children picked up on this enthusiasm. Bill relaxed enough that his behavior became less obnoxious. Eventually, Bill was a desired playmate.

3. Impart fairness and empathy. Our own relationships with teachers, parents, and children set the tone for children's relationships. A concerted, consistent, and continuous effort is needed to break down stereotypes, as demonstrated by efforts to encourage cross-sex cooperative play (Serbin, Tronick, & Sternglanz, 1977)—efforts that were only effective for the duration of the research. Children returned to their previous levels of play at the end of the project.

If a concentrated effort to change attitudes and practices only lasts as long as the treatment is in effect, think of the impotence of what Derman-Sparks et al. (1989) call the "tourist curriculum" that is intended (usually once a year) to deal with racial biases simply by teaching about cultures through holiday celebrations and cultural artifacts such as food, traditional clothing, and household implements.

> Tourist curriculum is both patronizing, emphasizing the "exotic" differences between cultures, and trivializing, dealing not with the real-life daily problems and experiences of different people, but with surface aspects of their celebrations and modes of entertainment. Children "visit" non-White cultures and then "go home" to the daily classroom, which reflects only the dominant culture. (p. 7)

We move, then, to recommendations for establishing an environment, at home or in programs, that is more in keeping with our knowledge about the development of self-worth in children.

Adults establish the environment

The richness of the preschool and kindergarten ages has recently been underplayed as more schools have resorted to academically-oriented programs (see Greenberg [1990] for the historical background of this phenomenon). Elkind (1987) points out the dangers of miseducating 5-year-olds: "When we push the first-grade curriculum into the kindergarten, we are imposing symbolic and derived learning experiences on children who, for the most part, are not ready for such experiences" (pp. 140–141). And frequently the former kindergarten curriculum has been pushed down into the preschool, so that even 3-year-olds are often found being drilled to learn the alphabet and count to 20.

An intriguing review of preschools in China, Japan, and the United States points out the varying foci of these programs (Tobin, Wu, & Davidson, 1989). The authors note that, while we in the United States ostensibly espouse a child-centered curriculum, many of our preschools stress academics, much as do the preschools in China. A fascinating discovery in this study is that Japanese preschools do *not* stress academics, but instead put a strong emphasis on the dispositions for learning (Katz & Chard, 1989): perseverance; skills in thinking, studying, and getting along with others; fostering a positive attitude toward school. This may give us one piece of the puzzle about why Japanese youth attain high achievement in their later school years.

If we are to contribute to children's emerging sense of self, however, the preschool curriculum, and the entire classroom setting, must be developmentally appropriate, including the **how** as well as the **what** of learning.

Design a balanced curriculum

Knowledge of child development, such as that presented here, forms the basis for tailoring a curriculum designed to meet children's needs, interests, and capabilities. This type of curriculum is espoused through the National Academy of Early Childhood Programs (see Bredekamp, 1987; Derman-Sparks et al., 1989). Guidelines for appropriate activities will be briefly reviewed here as they relate to children's development of self-esteem and beyond.

Activities that parents plan at home for their children are, in essence, the home curriculum. The same developmental principles apply there, in church school programs, in play groups, or wherever children gather.

1. Make the curriculum child-centered. This is easier said than done. The reality of many classrooms for preschool children, especially those under the direction of people with little professional preparation in early childhood education, is that a great deal of time is spent in child management (Bruner, 1980). Images of instructions, commands, and prohibitions, typical of the traditional teacher, and worksheets tackled by quietly sitting children, typical of the traditional classroom, are difficult to replace with more child-centered techniques.

Yet, if we are to deliver our promise to the development of children's self-esteem, changes are in order for most group programs. The curriculum is everything that happens during the day, including nap time, snack, outdoor play, as well as free play and group times.

A child-centered curriculum *is* the responsive conversations shared between adult and child, the atmosphere of delight in learning that is

Children are as eager to please each other as they are to please adults, sometimes even more so.

established, the thrill of discovering a beautiful book together, the singing of silly songs, the growing mastery of body and mind. It *isn't* agonizingly long circle times led by a teacher, or coloring books that deaden creativity, or unrealistic expectations about learning to read or count, or memorizing colors and shapes, or inappropriate performances such as graduation ceremonies.

The hallmarks of this type of curriculum, which includes the concept of scaffolding (support with challenge), are responsive conversation, asking open-ended questions, and facilitation of the child's initiatives. Goals for children's learning cover social, emotional, physical, and cognitive skills that are reasonable, given each child's age and abilities. Schedules are varied, taking into account that young children need to be active and involved. Children's eagerness to please enables teachers to tap into children's own interests and expand their experiences in meaningful ways.

Choices of activities—for problem solving, increasing skills, and inquiry—are abundant and varied. Children are respected as unique individual learners who learn best through self-direction and who are growing in self-regulation. But adults also take responsibility for assuring the underlying structure and direction that makes it all possible.

2. Plan for children's success. Activities, schedules, materials, and equipment must be selected to ensure that children will be both challenged and successful in their school experiences. Activities are hands-on, based on children's curiosity about themselves, each other, and the intriguing world. Children explore real things individually and in small groups, working alone and together. Their friendships are facilitated as they play together, comfort each other when the going gets rough, and assist each other when a puzzle is just too puzzling.

Children are also learning to control themselves. Nothing feels better than being able to use words to express emotions, rather than disintegrating into rage or sadness. Self-control is aided when expectations are based on children's development. Waiting is minimized. The schedule is fluid. Group times are short. Sharing is voluntary. Adults gently guide children through the ups and downs of growing up. Children learn to love themselves and each other—and feel good about what they can do—in developmentally appropriate programs.

Activities are selected to match variations of skills that exist in every group, so that all children can be competent at their own level. A good rule of thumb is this: *If the adult has to do most of the project, then it's not developmentally appropriate.* Another is this: *If all projects look alike, then they are not developmentally appropriate.* Adults set the stage for learning; they don't do it for the children by cutting, drawing, making models, or otherwise making the project their own more than the children's. Children's creations should be as unique as their personalities.

3. Enthusiastically involve yourself. The adults' attitudes spill over onto the children. As we saw with a bull-in-the-china-shop child, even a cheerful greeting can create remarkable changes in all the children in a group. This same sense of warm delight and fascination with learning should permeate the atmosphere.

More than that is required, though, to ensure that children experience a well-rounded curriculum. A balance of adult-directed and self-directed activities (Bruner, 1980; Wood, McMahon, & Cranstoun, 1980) lends the right amount of direction to learning.

> While it is true that an overly programmatic approach of an adult does depress children's interest and involvement, it is unlikely that no help at all is the right prescription either. Sharing the activity with an adult is often a good stimulus to enjoyment. . . . Added to this is the fact that without an adult's overall framework the child simply will not succeed in many of the tasks he sets himself. If he is to leave a task feeling competent and successful, then, he will often need the support of someone more knowledgeable than himself. (Wood et al., 1980, p. 114)

Knowing how to achieve this balance requires knowledge about children such as that reviewed here. Readers are referred to resources such as Katz and Chard (1989), DeVries and Kohlberg (1990), and Bredekamp (1987) for guidance. Inquiring minds flourish in an atmosphere and setting that supports self-esteem. Let us now see how the setting is structured to offer this support.

Plan an intriguing play area

The selection of materials, their arrangement, and the time allocated for their use all contribute to an environment that leads to a sense of competence and mastery. But it will only work if the adults are convinced of the value of children's making choices. Extremes — emphasizing academics or taking a helter-skelter approach — fail to support children's autonomy, initiative, and self-direction. Let's take a peek at an environment that *does* support these goals for children.

* * *

In this developmentally appropriate classroom, the teachers have erected a rich, inviting environment. Each interest area is labeled and has a related display. The housekeeping area is labeled as such, and includes a bulletin board "When I Grow Up I Want To Be" with a diversity of pictures of many professions. The nearby block area contains a variety of props to encourage different types of construction play, including

If we are to deliver our promise to the development of children's self-esteem, changes are in order for most group programs.

miniature people and various vehicles. Hard hats, briefcases, and every-day items representing many cultures are available, too.

In the table games area, commercial puzzles and manipulative toys are supplemented with home-made games. The arts and crafts area is amply supplied with markers, scissors, paste, fabric and yarn scraps, large sheets of paper, clay, and other do-it-yourself materials. All items are spread out on shelves, so children can select and then return the item of their choice. Tables are close by, or children can spread out on the floor. Children's artwork is hung at their level around the room.

The science corner includes magnifying glasses, shells, an empty wasp's nest, a balance, a book on insects, some houseplants, and a family of hamsters. Nearby are real musical instruments (tambourines, drums) and accessories for movement activities, such as scarves, so children can make as well as listen to beautiful sounds.

Children's literature is abundant in the cozy reading area, filled with soft pillows and covered with carpet so children can snuggle up with their favorite book. A writing area adjoins it, where children can construct their own books or prepare cards for a friend. Through the windows, we can see the outdoor play area, an amalgam of sun and shade, grass and sand, traditional swings and piles of tires, riding vehicles, and sand toys.

The teachers mingle with the children as they engage purposefully in the activity of their choice. The room is peaceful, with the low hum of conversation punctuated by laughter. Then it's cleanup time, followed by a brief gathering of the group to read a book about ice and pass around ice cubes. Children put on their coats, fill various containers with water to freeze, and head for the crisp outdoor air.

* * *

The principles illustrated in this classroom have a history beginning with Froebel (1987) and Montessori (1973), whose child-sized, self-correcting materials ensure that children's autonomy and initiative are addressed. A large body of literature has been developed by experts in preschool environments such as Olds (1979), Prescott and colleagues (1967, 1976, 1987), Moore (1980, 1985, 1986, 1987), and Moore and colleagues (1979). Harms and Gifford (1980) have developed instruments to evaluate early childhood environments.

These principles of environmental planning emerge again and again in the literature:

1. Design space to facilitate traffic flow and at the same time to protect children's need for quiet and undisturbed work. Access to several play areas stimulates interaction. Group together noisier areas (carpentry, housekeeping), quieter spaces (books, table toys), and messy activities (painting, pasting). Bathrooms should be readily accessible.

2. Provide child-size furniture and fixtures so children can be as independent as possible. Children learn just where to find (and replace) what they need when materials are displayed on low, open shelves. A big chair or sofa is good, too, for sharing a favorite book or cuddling up when children need a quiet hug.

3. Choose an ample variety of developmentally appropriate materials so children have real choices: carpentry, art, water and sand, blocks, props for pretend play, climbers, games, animals, plants, books, rocks, and fabric scraps offer countless possibilities for learning. Guide children's selection to help ensure challenges are coupled with success. Provide lots of options to spark interest in each area and to celebrate the diversity of our world. Rotate items as they are mastered or become old-hat.

4. Select materials with a variety of purposes in mind. Choose hands-on manipulatives that children can use in a variety of ways (blocks, dough clay). Self-guided materials (puzzles, form boards) enable children to immediately measure their levels of accomplishment.

5. Keep groups small to encourage cooperative play and self-control, and to minimize noise. Even field trips are more interesting when shared by a few children in a group, so that all can see, hear, and touch.

Thus, the human and the physical environment each play a crucial role in enhancing facets of children's self-esteem.

The form that interactions between preschooler and adults take—what type of activity they are involved in: the time available for chat, play, and teaching—is intimately bound up with the physical structure of the school, and the fit between the school and the school's philosophy and its architectural form. (Woods et al., 1980, p. 26)

In sum, we see that self-selection of activities that have been prepared and thoughtfully set up can enhance a child's sense of autonomy and initiative. Developmentally appropriate, adult-directed activities—provided the adult's goal is that of facilitation and not control for its own sake—can undergird mastery and a sense of competence. All of these factors enable preschoolers to feel virtuous and confident about themselves as they reach for the next step in their development.

Chapter 6

The kindergarten and primary years: Teaching children who are setting new standards for the self

THE PREVIOUS CHAPTERS HAVE DESCRIBED STRATEGIES FOR AND PITFALLS TO helping very young children achieve a healthy sense of self. With the new developmental tasks and challenges facing the school-age child, children will continue to benefit from behaviors that reflect high self-esteem as delineated by Haltiwanger in Table 4 (see pp. 62–63).

Yet, school counselors and child mental health specialists know that the number of children referred to them for treatment rises dramatically in the early school years, usually after the first report period, and in general the difficulties are related to school. This is not to say that the school creates these problems, but the symptoms of low self-esteem that may have been evident earlier (e.g., excessive fearfulness; difficulties with other children) now collide with school expectations.

As in earlier growth stages, there are developmental tasks being completed, tasks being consolidated, and new tasks to face. Entrance into kindergarten marks the beginning of a major life-cycle transition that children face in their own ways, given their unique background, talents, and personality. This is a key transition, but it is important to remember that most children have had some kind of group learning experience prior to kindergarten — ranging from a year of nursery school to 4 or 5 years in child care. These children, if exposed to developmentally appropriate practices as recommended in earlier chapters, are worldly wise veterans of an educational system that has encouraged their competence, acceptance, power and control, and moral virtue.

There has been a strong, well-meaning tendency to assume that some children are not ready for the new demands of school. As a result, children have been held back or placed in special developmental programs designed to enable them to mature. However, as described in Chapter 3, these strategies have not proven effective (Shepard & Smith, 1986). We can no longer justify holding children responsible for becoming ready.

Our schools must adjust to be ready to address the diverse needs of children. Being ready for these young children includes being prepared to deal with the variety of their individual talents and temperaments, their preschool experiences, and their family backgrounds and cultures.

The philosophy espoused here, as in earlier chapters, places a strong emphasis on recognizing individual differences in development and on helping children grow as valuable human beings. Against pressures that tend to focus attention on academic performance, it is important to emphasize the broader goals of education:

> . . . in advocating a developmentally appropriate orientation for programs, we believe the emphasis on youngsters as "students" — as only "cognitive systems" — should be converted to an emphasis on "children" as developing human beings, with as much attention given to the development of humane values (caring, consideration, concern, and thoughtfulness) as to the development of dispositions for learning (motivation, persistence, and thoroughness) of cognitive processes. (Kagan & Zigler, 1987, p. 22)

There has been little empirical research on aspects of schools that contribute to optimal self-development in general (Goebes & Shore, 1978), in part because such effects are more difficult to measure. Yet there is considerable literature that bears specifically on children's developing understanding and feelings of competence, power, social acceptance, and morality. Recommendations will be made for supporting positive developments in each of these important dimensions of self-evaluation.

Competence

Middle childhood is an important period for developing a sense of industry or competence. Children need to experience themselves as growing, learning, and developing in valued ways. At the same time, children inevitably come to recognize that all children have differing abilities. If self-esteem is based on beliefs about comparative ability, some children are bound to feel inferior; others will feel overly self-satisfied. In either case, further efforts toward achievement are compromised. We know that children who are gifted can be plagued with self-doubt, just as children with disabilities can feel good about their competence. The developmental task for all children is to evolve an honest sense of their own competencies that contributes to, rather than detracts from, their subsequent development.

Focus on the process of becoming competent

Chapter 3 described how children begin the school years believing that competence is an incremental process and that effort is related to ability: They can do better if they just try harder. Soon, however, they develop a second view of competence, seeing it as a fixed entity. Effort is viewed as the opposite of ability: The more effortless the accomplishment, the higher one's ability. Although there is validity to this second notion of ability (human abilities span a wide range), this is a debilitating criteria when applied to self-worth. The value of people should be measured in terms of *how* they use their talents, not in terms of *what* their talents are.

In their excellent book, *Coaching Young Athletes,* Martens, Christina, Harvey, and Sharkey (1981) summarize basic principles aimed at rewarding the incremental *process* of achieving rather than the *outcome:*

- Reward the performance, not the outcome.
- Reward athletes more for their effort than the actual success.
- Reward the little things along the way toward reaching the larger goal.
- Reward not only the learning and performance of sport skills, but also the learning and performance of emotional and social skills. (p. 42)

What do we mean by *reward?* How children are rewarded can make all the difference in whether children focus on the external trappings of success or develop more genuine commitments to personal and social improvement.

As we have seen, empty praise and extrinsic, ego-oriented rewards, such as stickers or ribbons, threaten to undermine genuine efforts toward developing competence. Children may come to see these rewards as bribes, or as collections to show off to others, or as something they expect regardless of how hard they try.

When ego-oriented rewards drive children, they lose interest in learning for its own sake. They tend to choose the easiest projects, the shortest books on which to report. They concentrate on what they can get out of their work—ice cream, $10, a book full of stickers. As teenagers and adults, they may continue to look for what they can get.

Instead, children can be praised, encouraged, and recognized for their genuine efforts, hard-won personal accomplishments, and valued social commitments. Such rewards support children's appreciation of the *intrinsic* rewards that come from improving their own performance, from figuring out the solution to a challenging problem, from learning something new, and from working together to accomplish a goal.

Task-oriented classrooms, as we have seen, help children focus on their own efforts, rather than comparing their work to others. These children experience joy in learning. They understand the value of cooperation. They are willing to take risks and to try new ideas. Teens and adults maintain these attitudes, too, in their work and at home, as well as in their education.

Avoid stereotypes and labels

Adults should never prejudge children's self-characteristics. We know that teachers place undue emphasis on children's age in judgments of readiness, and frequently misidentify children as having learning disabilities (Shepard & Smith, 1986). Sex stereotypes are also known to bias beliefs about children's competencies. Parents have been found to hold higher expectations of the math abilities of their sons than daughters, quite apart from their actual abilities. These differences predict that girls will have more disparaging attitudes toward math, and thus experience lower achievement in math in the high school years (Phillips & Zimmerman, 1990, p. 52).

Teachers' biases may have a particularly damaging effect on minority children. Entwisle and Alexander (1988) studied factors affecting achievement test scores and marks of African American and White first graders. Although the CAT test scores of both groups of children were similar, their parents' expectations were equally high, and they both studied the same curriculum, there were significant differences in the marks the children received in reading the first quarter of the year: African American children scored lower than the White children. "Furthermore, these first reading marks played a larger role in determining the later marks of Black than did the first reading marks of the White" (p. 468).

The authors concluded that teachers, more than parents, were the important others to the African American students, that absences and grade retention had more serious consequences for the African American students, and that "teachers judge the conduct of Black students who are relatively high achievers to be less satisfactory than that of Blacks who are not achieving as well" (p. 469).

Children who have real or supposed disabilities and behavior disorders are often assigned labels such as ADD (attention deficit disorder), mentally retarded, dyslexic, auditory learner, or hyperactive. As we saw in Chapter 3, such labels seem to focus adult attention on children's limitations, rather than on their strengths. Some children are even mislabeled. As educators we must turn our attention toward building children's strengths and finding ways to help them overcome obstacles. Passive learning environments, lavish but general praise, and token rewards, so common in special education, merely reinforce children's sense of helplessness.

Biases occur not only with respect to intellectual ability, but other characteristics as well. Consider the dangers of attributing artistic talent or creativity to children. Many adults remain incapable of drawing anything more than stick figures because they prematurely concluded that they weren't artistic or creative. Like intelligence, creativity is too often treated as a fixed trait, rather than as incremental processes. More than something you "have," creativity should be viewed as something that can be developed.

Instruct children in the hows of success

Teachers of younger children commonly reward effort more than ability. But this strategy is not sufficient. What about the child who doesn't try? The natural conclusion is that this child is lazy, but such a label is neither accurate nor helpful. Children do not try because they are not invested in the task and/or they do not know how to successfully mobilize their efforts for success.

Teddy seemed unable to apply himself. He was often daydreaming and expended little effort on his workbook assignments. His teacher and parents repeatedly told him, "You're not trying." "You need to work harder." These harangues, however, brought only temporary improvement. Soon Teddy was back to his old ways. Curiously, little effort was expended to teach Teddy how to apply himself, to help Teddy discover the intrinsic pleasures of learning, or to introduce more interesting learning activities. Teddy was learning that the effort and involvement that he lacked were fixed traits, rather than skills to be learned, and that school was dreadful. Teachers can use several strategies to foster the development of skills that lead to success.

Structure for success. No child should experience repeated failure in the classroom. Repeated failure is a sign that the educational program is inappropriate, not that the child is incompetent or lazy. This point is nicely made by Barbara Sizemore, a colleague at the University of Pittsburgh. She has studied the characteristics of schools where lower-SES African American children achieve high levels of academic success. Among other qualities, such schools are characterized by high goals, the clear expectancy that students will achieve these goals, and the supports needed for such achievement. As Sizemore (Crittendon, 1990) recently put it, such schools "monitored their [students'] achievement and set up pacing programs to help them catch up if they were behind. They [the students] weren't told 'You are behind because you're no good or your daddy is not good,' They were told, 'You are behind because your instruction was not well planned.' " (unpaged). Changes were then made in

The value of people should be measured in terms of how they use their talents, not in terms of what their talents are.

curriculum and teaching strategies to provide a better match with the students (see Sizemore, 1987, for details).

Teach strategic thinking. Education is fundamentally a matter of teaching students how to engage in strategic, planful actions aimed at valuable educational goals. Our goal is to develop self-directed, self-motivated, self-managed, self-regulated learners. To this end, programs developed specifically to train strategic thinking have been shown to enhance problem-solving skills as well as the desire to learn. Such training helps students discover that ability is not a fixed trait, but rather can be created or enhanced by means of learning how to better "use your head" (Covington, 1990). Similar successes have been demonstrated in teaching children social problem-solving skills (Strein, 1988).

How do children learn to solve problems? By tackling real situations in which they can become invested, not by answering word problems in math or finding simple answers in their reading books. Tests and worksheets lead children to believe that there is only one correct answer, when in fact for most problems there are many valuable solutions. Children need plenty of chances to generate possible answers, to experiment with those they think make the most sense, and to realize the consequences of their decisions.

Young children begin to learn problem-solving skills as they work out differences with each other and experiment with ways to solve a block building or collage dilemma. Older children use these same thinking skills to confront ever more complicated tasks. For example, a group of second graders might be working on a map of their school area. What should be included on the map? How big can the map be? What materials will be used? What committees are needed? Adults can help children frame important questions and encourage children to work together to come up with workable solutions.

Similarly, children can learn to solve social problems by coming up with possible alternatives (Shure & Spivack, 1978). Jenny, who is moving from a far-away state, will be coming to the third grade next week. What can the children do to help her feel welcome? At school? In the neighborhood? In the city?

Call attention to everyday situations that need solutions—How can we organize a field trip to the planetarium? What can we do about library books not being returned on time? Why are so many children being injured on the playground? When children are given opportunities to find solutions, they learn to think for themselves. They are indeed competent.

With this type of learning, math, science, reading, writing, art, and social studies all overlap and children recognize how useful they can be. Children become meaningfully involved in their learning.

Build commitment and task involvement. The best way to build a sense of industry is to successfully engage children in valuable pursuits. Children feel valued when they are engaged in a significant enterprise. Too often school is anything but engaging. As an 8-year-old put it to her 5-year-old brother who was apprehensive about beginning grade school, "But of course you're not supposed to like grade school. It's *supposed* to be worse than preschool."

Significant enterprises are easily found in any classroom. Use the ideas of scaffolding and project webs (Katz & Chard, 1989) to get started. How can our desks be arranged so that we are most productive? How can responsibilities for our plants, animals, sports equipment, lunch tickets, attendance, and other classroom tasks be shared? What can we do about litter in the hallways?

Curriculum goals in all areas can be met as children select interesting projects and carry them through.

- What do plants need to grow? How can we find out? How can we keep track of what happened? How can we apply what we know to the plants in our room? At home?

- Let's do a play for the younger children in the school: What kind of play would they like? What actors are needed? How can we choose who plays the roles? How do we make costumes and sets? What arrangements need to be made for programs, seating arrangements, and refreshments?

- We'll plan a heritage dinner for our parents. How can we find out where our ancestors came from? What foods did they like to eat? Where can we get the recipes and the ingredients? How will we raise the money to pay for the groceries? Who will print the invitations and menus? What do we need to prepare the feast? How will we clean up?

Pick up on the children's interests. Build on topics introduced in the established curriculum. Take charge of everyday problems. Make learning come alive for children!

Overcome the work-play dichotomy. Teachers, parents, and children alike too often view school activities in terms of work or play. Work is supposed to be the real business of school — it is required and serious — whereas play is spontaneous and fun (and the great advantage of preschool). Although teachers acknowledge the importance of play, it is typically relegated to a secondary role, as an activity after the "real work" is done (King, 1978).

Hence, the real business of school is portrayed as something unpleasant and to be avoided whenever possible, while play is viewed as a pleasant, self-chosen, but largely unproductive activity. The problem with this dichotomy is that it tends to preclude thinking that work can be a preferred, self-fulfilling activity, or that play can be boring and unpleasant (Sutton-Smith & Kelly-Byrne, 1984).

The sense of industry in middle childhood is best supported by activities that combine elements of work and play. The notion of *Flow* is one example. Flow is a state of intense task involvement that can be found in work and play. Flow occurs in self-chosen activities where there is an intense concentration of attention, a loss of self-consciousness, and a sense of being in control. Flow experiences have been described in such diverse activities as chess playing, surgery, and assembly line work (Csikszentmihalyi, 1979).

Projects such as those suggested in earlier sections of this chapter, hobbies, and sports similarly combine elements of both work and play. Adults promote children's development when they expect children to be deeply engaged in productive pursuits, rather than worrying about whether their activities are work or play.

Support intrinsic motivation

Children are involved and committed when activities are intrinsically rewarding. In school, our goal is to help children experience the intrinsic rewards of curiosity and wonderment, of helping others and solving social problems, and of self-improvement.

Of course, children may need considerable support, specific praise, and encouragement to eventually realize the intrinsic rewards of their efforts. Learning any new skill, whether it be reading, swimming, or soccer, often begins with a period of frustration and uncertainty, so frequent reassurance during this time is helpful. Some children also need more encouragement than others.

Researchers have found that teachers of high-SES children tend to offer little praise and mild criticism, whereas teachers of low-SES children and those with learning disabilities use more praise (Licht & Kistner, 1986). The reasons for these differences are not clear. In part they may show that teachers are being responsive to the legitimate needs of children. But as we have seen, children can become too dependent on external praise, and can benefit from appropriate criticism. Our goal is to develop children who appreciate the intrinsic pleasures from solving problems and expanding their abilities.

Most teachers recognize the importance of intrinsic motivation, but they often fail to recognize how their behavior may undermine it. One teacher we know is revered by children because she constantly lavishes them with rewards, presents, and praise. She has a reputation of being a warm and wonderful teacher. But, what is the educational message in this environment? The message is that education is a trivial pursuit, aimed at pleasing the teacher and getting trinkets.

Excessive praise and positive reinforcement put children at risk for lower self-esteem. As Hitz and Driscoll (1988) carefully point out, *encouragement,* which is task-oriented, is better than *praise* that is ego-oriented. Praise can be useful when it focuses on acknowledging children's *efforts* ("You sure are working hard"), but can backfire when it focuses comparative *ability* or *achievement.*

Send messages high in information. As Martens et al. (1981) carefully point out, good coaches provide specific information relevant to improving skills, as opposed to global judgments of praise or condemnation. For example, they discuss a study of the verbal communications of a famous coach of a college basketball team. Two psychologists found that 75% of his messages gave specific instructions, 12% consisted of requests to hustle, 7% were praise, and 6% were scolds. In another study, they note that Little League coaches who provided more instructions were evaluated more positively by players than coaches who gave general encouragement. This was particularly true for players who were low in self-esteem. Above all, these players wanted to know specifically how to improve their skills.

Help set appropriate personal standards

As children enter the school years, they begin to evaluate themselves according to new standards of achievement. They need considerable help in determining what appropriate standards are for themselves. Sometimes children set standards too high for themselves, and are then distraught by the slightest failure; other times standards set are too low, so children are satisfied with mediocre performance.

The intolerance many children have for their mistakes must not be overlooked when introducing children to new skills. Tonya, a first grader, began to develop stomachaches every Thursday. Her mother finally realized they occurred on gym days. With much probing, it turned out that Tonya, a perfectionist and a top student in math and reading, had heard the student teacher announce that they were going to learn to dribble the basketball in gym. Knowing there was no way she could do this higher level physical feat, Tonya agonized about her potential failure so much that her stomach *did* rebel. Fortunately, her mother was observant and could help Tonya begin to understand that perfection is not always necessary and that with practice, she could be an adequate, if not an outstanding, dribbler.

James (1890) argued that self-esteem is the ratio of success over pretention. An important task of middle childhood is to set the appropriate pretentions or standards of achievement. Standards that are too high will

The best way to build a sense of industry is by successfully engaging children in valuable pursuits.

result in frustration and feelings of defeat. Standards that are too low will result in self-satisfaction with little motivation for improvement.

Help develop differentiated self-concepts

As children undertake new challenges in the early school years, when they still have undifferentiated views of their competence, they are prone to extremes in self-evaluation. Some children defend the view that they are all smart (or lovable, or powerful, or good) whereas others defend the view that they are all dumb (hated, weak, or bad). From her clinical practice, Harter (1977) describes the following examples:

- A bright sensitive 7-year-old boy who had been diagnosed as dyslexic, was convinced that there was not a smart bone in his body. He felt that he was "all dumb."
- Another patient, a bright 6-year-old boy, was referred because of a tremendous problem of acting out aggressively both at home and at school, where he demonstrated extremely poor impulse control. He was convinced that he was "all bad" and that there was nothing commendable about his behavior.
- Another related manifestation is the tendency of some young children to vacillate from one extreme to the other. Even though today they may feel "all happy," tomorrow some event may cause a dramatic shift toward the opposite pole at which they can only express their strong feelings of anger. (pp. 418–419)

Such children need support in developing a more differentiated, realistic, and stable sense of self. Harter (1977) describes methods she used with a 6-year-old girl who viewed herself as all dumb. Through the use of role playing (with the adult acting as student) and drawings, this girl gradually was able to recognize that there were smart parts of herself too (see Figure 2).

Although teachers cannot be therapists, they can nonetheless be sensitive to extremes in children's self-feelings and take time to point out the many aspects of selves, encouraging children to maintain a more balanced perspective.

Power

Competence and power are closely intertwined issues in middle childhood. In the case of power, our goal is to ensure that children feel they are capable of exercising control over their behavior, rather than being helpless victims of forces beyond their control. Children who see themselves as victims regard their behavior as dependent upon external forces (external locus of control) or upon internal, fixed traits (low ability).

Figure 2. K's subsequent modifications of the smart-dumb drawing.

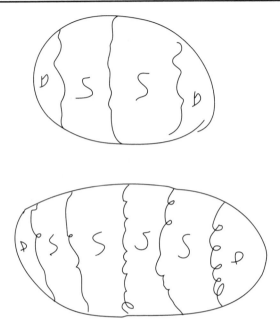

From "A Cognitive-Developmental Approach to Children's Expressions of Conflicting Feelings and a Technique to Facilitate Such Expression in Play Therapy" by S. Harter, 1977, _Journal of Consulting and Clinical Psychology, 45,_ p. 427. Copyright ©1977 by American Psychological Association. Reprinted by permission.

Power and competence are enhanced by methods described in the previous section, aimed at ensuring that children experience success in their active efforts to achieve personal valued goals. Other strategies are considered here.

Foster healthy competition

Concern about power raises the issues of competition, social comparisons, and status. As described in Chapter 3, the primary school years are characterized by strong tendencies toward comparing, competing, and ranking individuals according to their relative strengths, abilities, beauty, talents, or whatever. Not surprisingly, these tendencies are manifested in children's play as they begin to engage in formal competitive games.

Depending upon how they are directed, children's competitive tendencies can be either constructive or destructive. Appropriate competition can be an extremely powerful and positive mechanism to promote cooperation and self-development.

> Competition is neither good nor evil as such — it is merely a means by which we compare our abilities and efforts with others under agreed-upon issues. Whether competition is healthy depends on *how* we compete and the significance we place on winning. (Martens et al., 1981)

The key to healthy competition is to ensure that winning and ego-oriented success are made secondary to higher values of fairness, cooperation, and personal development. Good coaching, whether in sports or regular classroom activities, ensures that all children feel empowered with a larger, cooperative social enterprise (see Martens, Christina, Harvey, & Sharkey, 1981).

Competitive activities must be very carefully introduced in the early school years (see Kamii & DeVries, 1980; Passer, 1988). Children are just beginning to understand that winning and losing are all a part of the game (in play, like real life). Children need many low-pressure opportunities to explore this new domain of activity, where they can learn to playfully risk and tolerate defeat. "It" games are a particularly appropriate and popular kind of self-selected competition in the primary years. Games such as "Duck, Duck, Goose" and "Mother, May I?" help children deal with rivalry of powers in a playful, non-stressful manner. Unlike more complex team games where there are many different roles and one ultimate winner, It games have a simple role structure (It, not It) with no ultimate winner.

Appropriate competition also includes self-competition, with efforts directed toward improving one's own performance, or the performance of the class as a whole. And at ages 7 and 8, many children enjoy developmentally appropriate initiations into the world of team sports (Passu, 1988). Contrary to some reports of early stressful competition, sports organizations can and often do employ well-developed coaching practices that ensure positive experiences (see Martens et al., 1981).

Capitalize on strengths

Underscoring each child's strengths can be done in grade school as children come to recognize the excellent athlete, the socially competent child who can maintain group cohesion, and the exciting reader who can make a story line resonate with emotion.

Chuck, a boy with a mild, specific learning disability, held court as the neighborhood leader of about eight children (mostly younger) who adored him. They were intrigued by his novel play ideas and his enormous enthusiasm. He seemed undaunted by his mediocre academic performance and relished the powerful position he had at school and at home as the play initiator and leader. Every child has many strengths.

Astute teachers will recognize them and encourage children to build upon and expand their strengths.

Acceptance

Social relationships in the school-age child have been underscored as one of the hallmarks of this age. Having and being a friend occupies much of the school-age child's thinking and pursuits. The normal ups and downs of these relationships have been noted in Chapter 3, but persistent rejection poses a serious threat to children's sense of self. Children also continue to have a strong need for adult acceptance and approval, so negative teacher attitudes can seriously affect peer acceptance.

Teachers have a responsibility and the opportunity to assist children who are experiencing typical difficulties with peers. The following guidelines seem appropriate. For children with serious problems, teachers are urged to contact the school psychologist or other similar resource professional.

Respect children's social relations

Children's social relations should be taken seriously. The loss of a good friend can be a profoundly distressing event to a child. Adults need to be prepared to listen to and respect the growing depth of children's feelings. Rubin (1980) provides a good summary of the respectful approach needed with regard to supporting children's developing social skills:

Rather than "pushing" social skills indiscriminately, adults should respect the real differences between children that motivate some to establish friendly relations with many others, some to concentrate on one or two close friendships, and some to spend a good deal of time by themselves. Any of the patterns may be satisfying and appropriate to a particular child. Adults must also recognize that there are many personal attributes, some of them relatively immutable, which are likely to affect the way a child is viewed by his [or her] peers in a particular setting, including physical appearance, athletic prowess, intellectual abilities, and family background. As a result, different children may be best equipped with somewhat different skills of friendship. Finally, adults must be sensitive to events in children's lives that may underlie problems with making or keeping friends. Moving to a new school or neighborhood may create special difficulties, and so may stressful family events such as divorce. For the most part, children learn the skills of friendships not from adults, but from each other. But parents and teachers who are sensitive to individual children's distinctive needs and circumstances can facilitate this learning. (pp. 59–60)

The key to healthy competition is to ensure that winning and ego-oriented success are made secondary to higher values of fairness, cooperation, and personal development.

Break vicious cycles

Katz and Chard (1989) write of the recurring cycles children get into — that is, "once an individual has a given behavior pattern, reactions to him or her tend to elicit more of that behavior or characteristic" (p. 26). Moreover, children develop reputations that are often difficult to overcome.

Breaking such negative cycles requires intervention with both individuals and groups. The target individual needs specific coaching to change her behavior, while group dynamics must be modified to support these changes. Nelsen's (1987) guidelines for class meetings may be especially useful in working through these issues with children.

Coach social skills

Children who are rejected often suffer from poor social skills. It is not helpful to simply encourage such children to be nicer or more friendly. They need specific guidance on how to improve their social behavior.

Coaching techniques have been developed that have proved to be remarkably successful in improving social behavior (see Asher & Renshaw, 1981). These techniques variously include the following components:

1. Clarify the particular social concepts and behaviors that need to be addressed, such as the idea that aggression doesn't solve problems.
2. Discuss the concept and behaviors with children and consider alternative methods for problem solving.
3. Practice the skills through role-playing with classmates.
4. Coach children in the use of the concepts and behaviors in real situations.

Foster prosocial behavior. Prosocial behavior is fostered by giving high priority to social values and inducing children to think about the interpersonal consequences of their behavior. "How do you think Toby feels when you never let him play?" "What is it that annoys you?" "Is there a way we can solve this problem so Toby can play?" This is an area where teachers can work to model the behaviors they expect from children.

Avoid favoritism

Many grade school teachers reward quiet children for their passivity and shun the more rambunctious children, who come to see the teacher as an enemy, not an ally. We know a second grade teacher with an excellent reputation as a teacher of reading and as a fair disciplinarian. She makes allies of the children who come to her with reputations as "hell raisers." She selects them as her helpers, takes their hands on trips, and saves a seat beside her at story time, not as punishment but as an honor for herself. "I really like being with you" is her attitude, and the children respond with relief, mutual respect, and greatly improved behavior.

Observe behavior, especially at recess and lunch

The best and worst social behaviors occur in relatively unsupervised contexts, where teachers can note which children are bullying, which are being victimized, and which are maintaining solid friendships. Although children need opportunities to solve their own social problems, teachers need to monitor and intervene when children's solutions become persistently negative. An ethos of fairness, kindness, and respect should pervade school life, inside and outside the classroom.

Moral virtue

We have touched on the virtues of *goodness* and *badness* that children continue to struggle with. As mentioned in Chapter 3, fairness is the dominant moral standard for middle childhood. Teachers must be standard bearers for fairness. There are innumerable opportunities for teachers to demonstrate their own attitudes concerning fairness during the school day.

Treat children fairly

Teachers are not immune to biases that inevitably will influence their responses to children. There are some children who are very difficult to appreciate and accept, but as caring and sensitive adults we must monitor our responses. These children meet rejection everywhere, so teachers can devise strategies as mentioned here to help such children feel more accepted.

When they lack training and awareness, teachers are often biased in their attitudes and behaviors toward particular social groups. Teachers have been found to be remarkably unaware of the reality of racism (Milner, 1983) or unwilling to deal with it (Schofield, 1981). Both African American and White teachers have been found to have more negative perceptions of African American than of White children (Washington, 1982). Teachers also have been found to be less fair and understanding of lower-SES children (Hetherington, 1971). Age, abilities, and sex are other areas for monitoring our own fairness.

Teachers must examine their attitudes and work to modify them through self-examination, conferences with supervisors, and workshops to sensitize themselves to blind spots and prejudices (Derman-Sparks et al., 1989).

Treat children honestly

The need for constructive criticism implies that authenticity is essential in these years when children are developing a new sense of responsibility. Children are more astute than ever at picking up falseness and dishonesty from teachers. Fake and indiscriminate praise becomes meaningless to children, and they often mock the adult who uses it.

Expect individual responsibility

Children need to know that adults have standards. Their are times that children should feel guilty about their behavior, but adults need to induce guilt sparingly, for just causes, and with a good rationale. "How do you think he feels when you call him Fatso? How can you help him feel better?" is more effective than shaming a child.

Children need to gradually learn how to appreciate constructive criticism. Healthy people are open to criticism and change. There is no place whatsoever for shaming students, but teachers should hold children responsible for their actions.

> There is no more effective facilitator of moral development than fostering children's willingness to take responsibility for good and bad deeds. . . . This sense of responsibility goes to the heart of moral character—what was once called moral fiber. (Damon, 1988)

Although Americans often hurry children too fast into sports, dating, and the like (Elkind, 1981), there is no such hurrying toward moral and social responsibility. In fact, many American children seem to suffer from being given too little responsibility. Rather than believing that children must be shielded from real obligations for as long as possible, we need to do precisely the opposite: Entrust them with serious functions as soon as they are ready and able to perform them (Damon, 1988).

Children actually thrive on responsibility and take great pride in undertaking real jobs at which they do well: Under the pressure of reaching a deadline for this project, three young relatives, who were visiting the office, were pressed into service to help copy and collate the vast amount of material. The older child, age 10, ran the copy machine and the two younger children, ages 8 and 9, collated, stapled, and numbered the pages. The work pre-empted a planned boat trip, but the children were exhilarated by the challenge of helping us meet our deadline.

Changing the structure of classrooms

In large measure, self-esteem is supported by nothing more or less than *developmentally appropriate practices.* The strategies outlined here are undergirded by a child-centered philosophy with roots in the progressive school movement earlier in this century. Yet, despite numerous efforts toward reform, remarkably little has changed in the structure of most primary school classrooms. School life is still largely organized around a 19th century model of work: Like factory workers, children are trained to sit quietly, be well behaved, and work hard doing their piecework. It is assumed that some individuals will make it in the highly competitive world of work, whereas others will fail, largely due to their own lack of effort.

Most teachers recognize flaws in this value system, and espouse higher goals for education. Children need to be socialized to appreciate that learning, like work, is not passive, but active; not an individual enterprise, but a cooperative one; and not an onerous task, but a self- and socially fulfilling one. Covington (1989) summarizes these higher goals of education as:

- Satisfying one's curiosity and propagating a sense of wonder.
- Helping others or more broadly stated, committing oneself to solving society's problems.
- Mastery or self-improvement . . . becoming the best that one can be (p. 102).

Most teachers espouse these values, but major barriers must be overcome to implement them. Overwhelmed with pressures of mandated testing and problems with classroom management, many teachers end up rewarding children for little more than the mundane goals of listening to the teacher, doing their work, and not getting into trouble. Children are socialized into the passive role of student instead of the active role of learner. "I have no time to do interesting projects," complained a teacher, responding to a parent's concern that his child was bored. "We are mandated with certain curricular goals and our children are tested monthly to assess their progress. And children these days have so many problems. My goal is to help them develop good work habits."

Teachers often express this helplessness: What can I do, given these demands? Much can be done. Changing the reward structure of a classroom takes planning and preparation, but it also turns teaching and learning into a joy instead of a chore. Not only will children be more motivated, but they will achieve higher standards of performance.

How does one change the reward structure of a classroom? There are a variety of methods that Covington (1989) collectively describes as *equity structures.* The main idea is to *equalize* rewards and motivation for learning such that all students will experience the higher values of education, regardless of differences in actual ability and achievement. That is equal opportunity education with equity in diversity. What better way could there be to build upon schoolchildren's natural preoccupation with fairness?

There are a variety of equity structures that may be combined to meet different educational goals. Briefly, they include *cooperative learning,* where individuals achieve some standard of excellence to mark their own success by *contingency contracts,* in which students and teachers collaborate to set goals and rewards for self-directed learning. Or, standards may be set by the teacher, who aims children toward a given level of mastery. *Mastery learning* assumes that all students will succeed in achieving a given standard, regardless of ability, when given sufficient time, support, and practice (Covington, 1989).

There are many excellent statements about the principles of good early childhood education, most specifically NAEYC's *Developmentally Appropriate Practice in Early Childhood Programs Serving Children from Birth Through Age 8* (Bredekamp, 1987). We have chosen to focus on one specific methodology as an example of the way classrooms can be reorganized, namely Katz and Chard's (1989) *project method.*

Katz and Chard (1989) describe in depth the rationale and implementation of a method that echoes Bloom's proposal (1976) for teaching mastery learning.

> In a number of short-term studies compiled in his book, he shows the positive effect of mastery learning on the child's interest in subjects. According to Bloom this is because children's perceptions of themselves as adequate or inadequate in school affect their views of school and ultimately their sense of self. (Busch-Rossnagel & Vance, 1982, p. 458)

Katz and Chard (1989) have delineated four categories of learning goals that can be implemented through the project method:

1. Acquisition of knowledge. Teachers must understand "how children's knowledge develops and what they can understand as development proceeds" (p. 21). "While parents contribute informally and spontaneously to children's understanding, teachers are the adults in children's lives who undertake this role deliberately and intentionally (see Katz, 1984)" (pp. 21–22).

Teachers provide the structure for the acquisition of knowledge, tailoring it to children's developmental levels. Kindergartners who are studying about how houses are built might visit a construction site several times, write experience stories about what they saw, read *Building a House* (Barton, 1981), draw pictures or make models of the various stages of construction, and use simple carpentry tools such as hammers and saws.

Third graders would be led by their teacher to consider the topic more extensively. In addition to regular site visits, perhaps they would research the types of materials used; find out about local zoning and building codes; interview construction workers about their jobs; take photographs of the steps involved; and build self-selected, complex carpentry projects.

2. Acquisition of skills. "Skills are small units of action that can be fairly easily observed or inferred from observable behaviors" (Katz & Chard, 1989, p. 25). Children acquire many skills spontaneously, but adults still must guide learning of basic skills. Katz and Chard broaden the traditional view of academic skills to include social and communicative competencies.

The housing project, just described, enabled the children to put to good use and expand their skills in language, reading, math, science, art, social studies, and a host of other areas, none of which were fragmented.

3. Development of dispositions. Dispositions for learning are "relatively enduring habits of mind and action, or tendencies to respond to categories of experiences across classes of situations (Katz, 1985)" (Katz & Chard, p. 30). Here the authors are referring to dispositions such as "curiosity, resourcefulness, independence, initiative, responsibility, and other positive dispositions" (p. 30).

Teaching strategies such as the project method are aimed at building on these dispositions, for it is clear that we are educating children to live in a world whose challenges we can only imagine and for which flexible learning strategies will be essential. Consider how children can be encouraged when we use teaching strategies which stimulate positive dispositions:

- "How can we find out?" rather than "This is the way it is."
- "What will happen if . . .?" rather than "See what happens."
- "Who remembers when we mixed the newspaper and water and wrapped it around balloons? How are our projects different than they were yesterday?"
- "Why do we . . .?" rather than "Because I said so."

The enthusiasm and true curiosity of the teacher help keep alive the dispositions for learning cultivated in good preschools and homes.

4. Development of feelings. Katz and Chard (1989) mince no words about how teaching strategies affect a child's sense of self.

> In principle, when a young child's confusion, misunderstanding, misconceptions, and other difficulties do not cause the teacher to modify the instruction, vary the material, or otherwise to change her approach, the child may learn to feel helpless, hopeless, inadequate, and generally incompetent. Indeed, in such a situation the child *is* incompetent. (p. 40)

We cannot change children's abilities, but we can focus on their competencies, provide instruction to advance their competence, and recognize the feelings aroused when a child is made to feel incompetent ("*Another* mistake! When will you learn?"), powerless ("No recess for you! You must practice your numbers"), friendless ("Navaughn can't play here any more. He's too wild for you"), and bad ("That's the third time you hit Marcus. Shame on you. Wait till I tell your mother how bad you are!"). How easy it is to find examples of destructive—but common—teaching and parenting practices.

With the kinds of challenges projects provide for children, disruptive behavior lessens as interest rises. Enforced passivity results in acting-out behavior. The program is at fault, yet the child is left to feel bad.

Combine teaching strategies

Here is another example of how the project approach takes form:

In a developmentally oriented kindergarten the children began to spontaneously play haunted house in the block corner. They designed the walls of the house with large blocks, through which they wove their way on a small wheeled platform. They decided to draw scary pictures to put on the walls of the haunted house and added hand-printed signs, for which some needed help with the spelling in "Beware of the Ghosts" and "Monsters over here!"

Then they decided to charge admission and carefully made out tickets and pretend money. One of the children was ticket seller and another was ticket taker; both used their counting skills, as did the children creating the tickets and money. Although this began with one group of children, the whole class soon got caught up in it. One group took on the refreshment stand and the usual snack time was incorporated into the play, with children buying their juice and crackers with the pretend money they made.

This spontaneous project used the dispositions for learning deemed necessary by Katz and Chard (1989, p. 31)—simultaneous acquisition of knowledge (amusement parks are a part of most children's experiences), skills (beginning reading, writing, and math), desirable dispositions (enthusiasm, initiative, autonomy, cooperation, and social competence), and feelings (this project was a lot of fun and a source of gratification for everyone).

In conclusion, we believe that self-esteem is best supported in middle childhood by getting children involved in valuable pursuits. Attention should be focused on how to restructure classrooms in order to more fully and equitably engage each child in the higher values of education and work. In the process, children will experience themselves in genuinely valuable ways, as active learners, social problem solvers, and developing human beings. Teachers can take the opportunity to help children sift through a multitude of rich self-experiences, including both successes and failures, to develop a realistic, yet optimistic, sense of who they are and what they can become.

Chapter 7

Summary and implications
for policy

HAVING READ THIS BOOK, SOME PRACTITIONERS ARE BOUND TO SAY, "So what! We knew this!" In part this is true. Many excellent early childhood educators have known intuitively, and from their readings and experiences, which practices do or don't enhance self-esteem.

But knowing is different from knowing that we know. To the extent that our knowledge has been intuitive, our field has been vulnerable; we are accused of espousing soft science. Most of us have, at one time or another, sputtered and retreated (with lowered self-esteem!) under the barrages of "But where's your data?" We hope that some of the research cited in this book will buttress the excellent intuitions which have guided and should continue to inform our practices with young children.

Early childhood educators can feel justifiably proud and confident about a tradition that has long emphasized the importance of children's developing sense of self. Yet, it would be a mistake to feel self-satisfied. We must admit that we often have been guilty of exceedingly vague pronouncements about the importance of self-esteem. And practices have rarely lived up to ideals. Sensitivity to the inner needs of children has often been sacrificed to the external pressures for achievement and classroom management. We hope this monograph will inspire self-examination; what do we mean by *self-esteem,* and how well do we in fact implement supportive practices?

We have attempted to avoid the common mistake of isolating self-esteem from the larger context of children's — or our own — lives. And we have insisted that self-esteem is not a trivial pursuit that can be built by pepping children up with empty praise, extra pats, and cheers of support. Such efforts are temporary at best, and deceptive at worst. Our children need coaches, not cheerleaders. They need parents and professionals who know the game and can engage and guide children in the serious and playful business of growing up.

153

The goal of this volume has been to take us — parents, teachers, administrators, policy makers — beyond naive conceptions of self-esteem as an isolated entity, and toward understanding self-esteem as a dynamic, multidimensional phenomenon that must be viewed in the larger context of children's social, cognitive, moral, and personality development. Children are active participants in their developing sense of self, acting and interpreting what they do and what happens to them. Love and trust, power, autonomy, limits, initiative and morality, industry and competence, as well as sociability, self-control, and persistence, all play a compelling, lasting role in how children feel about themselves as people.

Self-esteem is a complex and elusive phenomenon. We have long recognized the importance of people's thoughts and feelings about themselves, but we are just beginning to understand how these thoughts and feelings actually develop. New methods and measures are providing the first-hand scientific basis for our intuitions.

New research inspires both confidence and humility. There is no doubt about the central importance of children's developing thoughts and feelings about themselves. And we can be assured that self-esteem is supported by developmentally appropriate practices. Yet we still know so little about the elusive and many-sided phenomenon of self. There is no simple way in which children can be inoculated with positive self-esteem.

In summary, we will sketch our major foundations, and the general implications from the research, with some broad recommendations to policy makers based on what we currently know about what leads to development of a healthy sense of self.

Major foundations

1. Beyond intuitions and global measures of self-esteem, current research provides a more detailed picture of the multi-faceted phenomenon of self-esteem.

   - Self-esteem is integrally related to the development of values and moral character, as well as the development of personality.
   - Concepts and feelings about the self develop in conjunction with the social, cognitive, moral, and personality development of the child.
   - Four major aspects of self-evaluations are acceptance, power/control, competence, and moral virtue.

2. Children develop self-understanding through collaboration with significant others, from which they construct a sense of self and a sense

of the value of that self. From birth children are an active part of a system that includes the social and cultural context of the family and the wider world.

- The processes of attachment and separation-individuation are integral to the development of the self in relation with others: parents, siblings, peers, caregivers, and teachers.
- Self-esteem is a lifelong developmental process, not a static entity, which has its roots in the developing and consolidating of the sense of self in early childhood.
- Children are active participants in the development of their sense of self, cognitively and behaviorally. Self-esteem does not simply mirror values and expectancies of others.
- Self-esteem develops in the context of changing life tasks and challenges.
- Children develop senses of resilience, power, competence, trust, and optimism from repeated experiences in which they transform negative states into positive ones.
- Persistently positive, as well as persistently negative, self-feelings place children at risk. The danger here lies in the narcissistic self-absorption of children who have not received authentic feedback and are ill-equipped to face the very real challenges of school and peer expectations.
- Peer relationships and adult-child relationships provide different contexts and different standards of self-evaluation.

Implications

Part of this book emphasizes specific practices designed to address self-esteem issues. Practitioners can be guided by the general principles which have emerged from informed practice and research.

- General standards of practice need to be upgraded, consistent with NAEYC's guidelines for developmentally appropriate practice that are undergirded by the research cited here.
- Self-esteem is supported by optimally balancing high nurturance and support with appropriately high standards, challenges, and restrictions. The concepts of scaffolding, authoritative parenting, and optimal frustration all provide models of this balance. Thus, parents and care-

givers may place toys slightly out of reach of babies, but also supply a lap on which the babies can play with these toys. Grade school teachers individualize reading by providing a variety of literacy experiences (dictated stories, diaries, stop-and-read times during the day in which children can choose books) with all children expected to participate at their own levels.

- Self-esteem is supported by generally good standards of practice (such as those espoused by NAEYC), not by special booster techniques, such as offers of pizza for reading a certain number of books per month.

- Self-esteem is supported by teaching children in skills and problem-solving techniques needed to achieve personally desired goals. Techniques that enable children to become strategic thinkers and social problem solvers need to be more widely understood and implemented.

- Different aspects of self-esteem — love and acceptance, power and control, competence and moral virtue — must be supported in different ways. For example, the need for adult love and acceptance is absolutely essential for babies; by school age, unconditional positive regard must be tempered with fair and honest evaluations of what is acceptable and why. Autonomy assertions in toddlerhood are a part of self-definition; grade-school children need the freedom to exercise their autonomy in approaching learning tasks.

- Practitioners should be sensitive and responsive in dealing with children's thoughts and feelings about themselves. Teachers and other caregivers need to see that children's learning and behavior is strongly affected by these thoughts and feelings. They need to help children interpret self-experiences, collaborating to develop authentic, adaptive self-understanding.

- Self-esteem is best supported by engaging children in valuable, intrinsically challenging enterprises. The project method of teaching, in which children and teachers work together on a project, is an ideal vehicle for integrating skills, knowledge, dispositions for learning, and feelings.

- Most primary school classrooms need to be restructured, using various equity structures, so that all children can experience the higher values and intrinsic rewards of education: discovery, helping others, and self-improvement.

- Teachers need better preparation and support to enable them to respond to the diverse individual needs of children entering school.

- Rewards should be task-oriented, encouraging effort and self-improvement. Ego-oriented praise and extrinsic rewards are not good ways to build self-esteem. Letter grades should not be used with early grade school children; rather, they need differentiated reports shared at intervals with parents, as is the practice in many fine preschools.

- Classrooms need to be guided by clear values that emphasize the special identity of each individual in conjunction with her or his ability to contribute to the larger social good. Such values are best taught in practice, through genuine experiences, rather than by empty preaching or abstract discussions. Anti-bias materials and activities, as outlined by the Anti-Bias Curriculum, are highly recommended (Derman-Sparks et al., 1989). Rich learning experiences should be embedded in the everyday structure of the center rather than a once-a-year token recognition, for example, of Martin Luther King, Jr.
- Efforts should be made to match teachers' personalities and training with age characteristics of children. All teachers and other caregivers should have a strong background in child development with early childhood teachers trained in methodologies emphasizing a developmental understanding of skill and knowledge acquisition.
- The ethos of all classrooms should be marked by an emphasis on the values of mutual respect, cooperation, empathy, and fairness. Classrooms need to be structured to ensure that teachers have opportunities to respond to, discuss, and model these values. Careful monitoring must ensure that instances of cruelty, prejudice, and victimization are addressed and eliminated.
- Authenticity and specificity in response to children should guide caregivers and teachers in their work with children. Honest feedback to specific behaviors helps children grow and change more than do global comments such as "good job."
- In-service and during-service activities for teachers and principals should be designed to focus on ways to enhance the various aspects of self-esteem (affection, power/control, competence, and moral virtue), rather than attempting to address self-esteem as a global entity to be elevated by praise and other extrinsic rewards.
- No children should be in an environment where they persistently experience themselves as failing, unaccepted, powerless, or bad.
- No children should be in an environment where they are persistently rewarded and praised for trivial activities as if they were in happiness factories.

Implications for policy and research

What general policies should be implemented to support the development of self-esteem? This question ultimately leads to fundamental considerations of our values and priorities as a society. How can we ensure that all individuals are given the support, guidance, and opportunities

Children are active participants in their developing sense of self.

essential for the development of a healthy sense of self? This issue was the focus of *Toward a State of Esteem* (California Task Force, 1990). This task force examined the role of self-esteem in the contexts of child maltreatment, failure in schools, teenage pregnancy, crime and violence, chronic welfare dependency, and alcohol and drug abuse. Although self-esteem is not the simple or direct cause of these societal ills, this book indicates the broad steps that must be taken to transform how we care for individuals in our society.

In recognizing the magnitude of the problem, it is important not to be overwhelmed by it. There is a temptation to suggest that we need more of everything — money, programs, training, salaries, and so forth — to address the problems of self-esteem (which is true), but we prefer to emphasize the importance of smaller, local steps toward change. As they say in the environmental movement, "Think globally, act locally." In this regard, Covington (1990) argues that change is most likely to occur when local groups work cooperatively to solve specific social problems:

> Benefits are most likely to result when the target group — say, school-aged children in a particular community — is immersed in a circle of positive, interlocking influences in the form of parental health education programs, church-based outreach groups, and community service organizations. Only by harnessing a number of preventive and promotion strategies in pursuit of a single goal will we have much reason for optimism about solving the many chronic and costly social problems that threaten the well-being of our citizens. And, in the last analysis, perhaps the most unifying and worthy goal is the promotion of feelings of individual and collective esteem. (p.111)

In fundamental ways we have long known what constitutes quality care. Currently there is an abundance of literature describing successful methods of practice. It is time to get our acts together. Much can be accomplished by practitioners who not only espouse the value of self-esteem, but also take concrete steps to ensure better practices to support it.

Self-esteem can be an organizing theme for all kinds of program changes aimed at improving early childhood education. One could target parents, emphasizing parental needs for support as well as skills in developing positive attachments, supportive scaffolding, and authoritative discipline with their children. Teachers also need more support and skills. Education, supervision, workshops, in-service programs, and salaries all need to be improved toward the goal of increasing professional competence.

More specifically, we recommend that practitioners begin by examining their own programs — in schools, churches, hospitals, Head Start, child care, family-based child care, home-based programs, government agencies, teacher education institutions, and elsewhere — to see if they are implementing practices that foster healthy self-esteem. Self-esteem

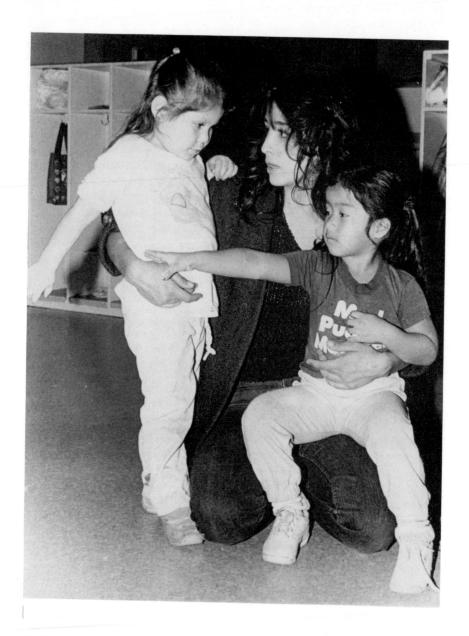

Children develop senses of resilience, power, competence, trust, and optimism from repeated experiences in which they transform negative states into positive ones.

is an excellent topic to organize thinking and assessments of practice. Many programs already include self-esteem as a primary objective. It is worthwhile, we think, to reconsider this objective, being careful to go beyond platitudes and overgeneralizations to consider specific issues and practices. We found one method to be very useful in fostering our own thinking. We asked teachers to select a child in their classrooms whom they believed had low self-esteem. Group discussion then focused around the behaviors that indicated low self-esteem, the seeming causes, and the practices that were being used or could be used to alleviate it. One such discussion led to the following insights: "Self-esteem is like an abbreviation for everything that's going on there." "Thinking about self-esteem as either high or low misses all the middle." "There are some children that show just certain things [negative], but when you sit down and look at the child as a whole, she does other [positive] things." "Praise doesn't strengthen his good behavior, it abbreviates it."

We know that there is often a wide gap between ideals and reality. Practitioners commonly acknowledge the importance of being sensitive and responsive to the individual needs of children, and most believe that they in fact are. But when given a chance to examine their actual practices, they may be surprised at how much their interactions are dominated by directing and telling children what to do, and how little time is spent listening, conversing with, and responding to the initiatives of children (see King, 1978; Wood et al, 1980). We suggest that teachers take the time to write down (or tape) their interactions with children for a short period of time, and then reflect on the quality of those interactions. Because this poses a potentially serious threat to teachers' self-esteem, we suggest that this be done privately or under very supportive conditions, with the idea of implementing some specific strategies for their own improvement, such as decreasing management demands, increasing teacher autonomy, and structuring opportunities for authentic interactions with children.

We also recommend that administrators pay particular attention to the reward structures of their programs, not just the rewards for children, but for teachers as well. To empower children, teachers need to feel empowered themselves. They, too, need the opportunities, support, and coaching necessary to achieve personally valued goals.

With regard to research, we hope this book will inspire a sense of both confidence and humility: confidence that we are finally on the right track; humility about how little we still know. Although we have tried to provide a more accurate picture of the complex issues surrounding self-esteem, we realize that we have often oversimplified the issues and ignored important variables. Much research remains to be done and must be integrated to guide practitioners. We are only just beginning to develop methods to assess the self-understanding of young children. Our understanding is often tentative and crude. Particularly missing is a more elaborate picture of the different ways that children may develop self-esteem, as well as different individual styles of coping. How is self-esteem fostered in different ethnic and social groups? What about sex differences? Are praise and external rewards more useful for certain groups of children? We need to know much more about how the same practices may yield different results with different individuals.

Clearly, we are espousing goals aimed at the very heart of human values and aspirations. Our hearts have long been in the right place. It is important now to combine big hearts with hard heads. We need to better understand what we feel, and to take manageable, coordinated steps aimed at achieving specific goals.

References

Abrams, S., & Neubauer, P. (1976). Object orientedness: The person or the thing. *Psychoanalytic Quarterly, 45,* 73–79.

Ainsworth, M.D.S. (1972). Attachment and dependency: A comparison. In J.L. Gewirtz (Ed.), *Attachment and dependency* (pp. 97–137). Washington, DC: Winston.

Ainsworth, M.D.S., Blehar, M.C., Waters, E., & Wall, S. (1978). *Patterns of attachment: A psychological study of the strange situation.* Hillsdale, NJ: Erlbaum.

Alexander, K.L., & Entwisle, D.R. (1988). Achievement in the first 2 years of school: Patterns and processes. *Monographs of the Society for Research in Child Development, 53,* 2.

Als, H. (1979). Assessing an assessment: Conceptual considerations, methodological issues and a perspective on the future of the Brazelton Neonatal Behavioral Assessment Scale (BNBAS). In A. Sameroff (Ed.), *Organization and stability of newborn behavior. A commentary on the Brazelton Neonatal Behavioral Assessment Scale* (pp. 1–10). *Monographs of the Society for Research in Child Development, 43*(5–6, Serial No. 177).

Als, H., Tronick, E., Adamson, L., & Brazelton, T.B. (1976). The behavior of the full-term but underweight newborn infant. *Developmental Medicine & Child Neurology, 18,* 590–602.

Als, H., Tronick, E., & Brazelton, T.B. (1980). Affective reciprocity and the development of autonomy: The study of a blind infant. *Journal of the American Academy of Child Psychiatry, 19,* 22–40.

Arend, R., Gove, F., & Sroufe, L.A. (1979). Continuity of individual adaptation from infancy to kindergarten: A predictive study of ego-resiliency and curiosity in preschoolers. *Child Development, 50,* 950–959.

Arnaud, S.H. (1972). Polish for play's tarnished reputation. In G. Engstrom (Ed.), *Play: The child strives toward self-realization* (pp. 5–12). Washington, DC: NAEYC.

Asher, S.R., & Gottman, J.M. (Eds.). (1981). *The development of children's friendships.* New York: Cambridge University Press.

Asher, S.R., & Renshaw, A.D. (1981). Children without friends: Social knowledge and social skill training. In S.R. Asher & J.M. Gottman (Eds.), *The development of children's friendships* (pp. 273–296). New York: Cambridge University Press.

Ayers, W. (1989). *The good preschool teacher.* New York: Teachers College Press.

Bailey, D.B., & Wolery, M. (1984). *Teaching infants and preschoolers with handicaps.* Columbus, OH: Merrill.

Bailey, R.A., & Barton, E.C. (1982). *The dynamic self: Activities to enhance infant development.* St. Louis, MO: Mosby.

Bandura, A. (1986). *Social foundations of thought and action.* Englewood Cliffs, NJ: Prentice-Hall.

Barnett, M.A., Howard, J., Melton, E.M., & Dino, G.A. (1982). Effects of inducing sadness about self or other on helping behavior in high- and low-empathic children. *Child Development, 53*(4), 920–923.

163

Barnett, M.A., King, L.M., Howard, J.A., & Dino, G.A. (1980). Empathy in young children. Relation to parents' empathy, affection, and emphasis on the feelings of others. *Developmental Psychology, 16,* 243–244.

Barton, B. (1981). *Building a house.* New York: Greenwillow.

Baumrind, D. (1971). Current patterns of parental authority. *Developmental Psychology Monographs, 4* (1, part 2).

Baumrind, D. (1979). *Sex-related socialization effects.* Paper presented at the biennial meeting of the Society for Research in Child Development, San Francisco.

Becker, W.C. (1964). Consequences of different kinds of parental discipline. In M.L. Hoffman & L.W. Hoffman (Eds.), *Review of child developmental research, 1* (pp. 169–208). New York: Russell Sage Foundation.

Bell, S.M., & Ainsworth, M.D.S. (1972). Infant crying and maternal responsiveness. *Child Development, 43,* 1171–1190.

Belsky, J., Lerner, R.M., & Spanier, G.B. (1984). *The child in the family.* New York: Random House.

Blank, M.B., Rose, S., & Berlin, L. (1978). *The language of learning: The preschool years.* New York: Grune & Stratton.

Block, J.H., & Block, J. (1980). The role of ego-control and ego-resiliency in the organization of behavior. In W.A. Collins (Ed.), *Development of cognition, affect, and social relations* (pp. 39–101), *Minnesota Symposium on Child Psychology,* Vol. 13. Hillsdale, NJ: Erlbaum.

Bloom, B.S. (1976). *Human characteristics and school learning.* New York: McGraw-Hill.

Bowlby, J. (1969). *Attachment and loss: Vol. 1, Attachment.* New York: Basic.

Bowlby J. (1973). *Attachment and loss: Vol. 2, Separation.* New York: Basic.

Bowlby, J. (1980). *Attachment and loss: Vol. 3, Loss, sadness, and depression.* New York: Basic.

Bowlby, J. (1982). *Attachment and loss: Vol. 1, Attachment (2nd ed.).* New York: Basic. (Original work published 1969)

Brazelton, T.B. (1989). Neonatal assessment. In S.I. Greenspan & G.H. Pollock (Eds.), *The course of life, Vol. 1, Infancy,* (pp. 393–431). Madison, CT: International Universities Press.

Brazelton, T.B., & Als, H. (1979). Four early stages in the development of mother-infant interaction. *Psychoanalytic Study of the Child, 34,* 349–370.

Brazelton, T.B., & Cramer, B.G. (1990). *The earliest relationship: Parents, infants, and the drama of early attachment.* New York: Addison-Wesley.

Brazelton, T.B., Koslowski, B., & Main, M. (1974). Origins of reciprocity. In M. Lewis & L. Rosenblum (Eds.), *The effect of the infant on caregivers* (pp. 49–76). New York: Wiley.

Bredekamp, S. (1987). *Developmentally appropriate practice in early childhood programs serving children from birth through age 8* (rev. ed.). Washington, DC: NAEYC.

Bredekamp, S. (1990). Extra-year programs: A response to Brewer and Uphoff. *Young Children, 45* (6), 20–21.

Bredekamp, S., & Shepard, L. (1989). How to best protect children from inappropriate school expectations, practices, and policies. *Young Children, 44* (3), 14–24.

Bretherton, I. (1985). Attachment theory: Retrospect and prospect. In I. Bretherton & E. Waters (Eds.), Growing points of attachment theory and research. *Monographs of the Society for Research in Child Development, 50* (1–2), 3–35.

Bretherton, I., Ridgeway, D., & Cassidy, J. (1990). The role of internal working models in the attachment relationship: Can it be studied in 3-year-olds? In M. Greenberg, D. Cichetti, & E.M. Cummings (Eds.), *Attachment during the pre-*

school years: Theory, research and intervention. Chicago: University of Chicago Press.

Brewer, J.A. (1990). Transitional programs: Boon or bane? *Young Children, 45* (6), 15-18.

Bridges, K. (1931). *Social and emotional development of the preschool child.* London: Kegan Paul.

Bronson, W.C. (1975). Developments in behavior with age mates during the second year of life. In M. Lewis & L.A. Rosenblum (Eds.), *Friendship and peer relations* (pp. 131-152), New York: Wiley.

Brown, J., & Helper, R. (1976). Stimulation — corollary to physical care. *American Journal of Nursing, 76,* 578-581.

Bruner, J. (1980). *Under 5 in Britain.* Ypsilanti, MI: High/Scope.

Buhler, C. (1935). *From birth to maturity.* London: Routledge & Kegan Paul.

Busch-Rossnagel, N.A., & Vance, A.K. (1982). The impact of schools on social and emotional development. In B.B. Wolman (Ed.), *Handbook of developmental psychology.* Englewood Cliffs, NJ: Prentice-Hall.

California Task Force. (1990). *Toward a state of esteem.* Sacramento: California State Department of Education.

Campbell, S. (1990). *Behavior problems in preschool children: Developmental and clinical issues.* New York: Guilford Press.

Cannella, G.S. (1986). Praise and concrete rewards: Concerns for childhood education. *Childhood Education, 62*(4), 297-301.

Cassidy, J. (1988). Child-mother attachment and the self in 6-year-olds. *Child Development, 59*(1), 121-134.

Chapple, E. (1970). Experimental production of transients in human interactions. *Nature, 226,* 630-634.

Chess, S., & Thomas, A. (1987). *Know your child: An authoritative guide for today's parents.* New York: Basic.

Cicchetti, D., & Sroufe, L.A. (1976). The relationship between affective and cognitive development in Down's syndrome infants. *Child Development, 46,* 920-929.

Clarke-Stewart, A., & Friedman, S. (1987). *Child development: Infancy through adolescence.* New York: Wiley.

Coie, J.D., & Dodge, K.A. (1988). Continuities and changes in children's social status: A 5-year longitudinal study. In E.M. Hetherington & R.D. Parke (Eds.), *Contemporary readings in child psychology* (pp. 477-488). New York: McGraw-Hill.

Collard, R. (1979). Exploration and play. In B. Sutton-Smith (Ed.), *Play and learning* (pp. 45-56). New York: Gardner.

Collins, W.A., & Gunnar, M. (1990). Social and personality development. In M.R. Rosenzweig & L.W. Partner (Eds.), *Annual Review of Psychology, 44,* 387-416.

Connell, J.P., & Ilardi, D.C. (1987). Self-system concomitants of discrepancies between children's and teacher's evaluations of academic competence. *Child Development, 58,* 1037-1297.

Coopersmith, S. (1967). *The antecedents of self-esteem.* San Francisco: W.H. Freeman.

Corsaro, W.A. (1985). *Friendship and peer culture in the early years.* Norwood, NJ: Ablex.

Covington, M.V. (1987). Achievement, motivation, self-attributes and exceptionality. In J.D. Day & J.G. Borkowski (Eds.), *Intelligence and exceptionality: New directions for theory, assessment and instructional practices* (pp. 173-213). Norwood, NJ: Ablex.

Covington, M.V. (1990). Self-esteem and failure in school: Analysis and policy implications. In A.M. Mecca, N.J. Smelser, & J. Vasconellos (Eds.), *The* social importance of self-esteem (pp. 72-124). Berkeley: University of California Press.

Cowen, E.L., Pederson, A., Babigian, H., Izzo, L.D., & Trost, M.A. (1973). Long-term follow-up of early detected vulnerable children. *Journal of Consulting and Clinical Psychology, 41*(3), 438-446.

Craik, K. (1943). *The nature of explanation.* New York: Cambridge University Press.

Crawley, S.B., Rogers, P., Friedman, S., Jacabbo, M., Criticos, A., Richardson, L., & Thompson, M. (1978). Developmental changes in the structure of mother-infant play. *Developmental Psychology, 14*, 30-36.

Crittendon, D. (1990, January 21). Education: Support helps poor Blacks achieve. *Detroit News and Free Press.*

Csikszentmihalyi, M. (1979). The concept of flow. In B. Sutton-Smith (Ed.), *Play and learning* (pp. 257-274). New York: Gardner.

Cunningham, E.E., Reuler, R., Blackwell, J., & Deck, J. (1981). Behavioral and linguistic developments in the interactions of normal and retarded children with their mothers. *Child Development, 52*, 62-70.

Curry, N.E., & Arnaud, S.H. (1974). Cognitive implications in children's spontaneous role play. *Theory into Practice, 13*(4), 273-277.

Curry, N.E., & Arnaud, S.H. (1984). *Play in developmental preschool settings.* In T.D. Yawkey & A.D. Pellegrini (Eds.), *Child's play: Developmental and applied* (pp. 273-290). Hillsdale, NJ: Erlbaum.

Curry, N.E., & Bergen, D. (1987). The relationship of play to emotional, social, and gender/sex role development. In D. Bergen (Ed.), *Play as a medium for learning and development* (pp. 107-132). Portsmouth, NH: Heinemann.

Cushman, P. (1990). Why the self is empty. Toward a historically situated psychology. *American Psychologist, 45*, 599-611.

Damon, W. (1988). *The moral child.* New York. Free Press.

Damon, W. (Ed.). (1989). *Child development today and tomorrow.* San Francisco: Jossey-Bass.

Damon, W., & Hart, D. (1982). The development of self-understanding from infancy through adolescence. *Child Development, 53*, 841-864.

DeLoache, J.S. (1987). Rapid change in the symbolic function of very young children. *Science, 238*, 1556-1557.

Derman-Sparks, L., and the A.B.C. Task Force. (1989). *Anti-bias curriculum: Tools for empowering young children.* Washington, DC: NAEYC.

DeVries, R., & Kohlberg, L. (1990). *Constructivist early education: Overview and comparison with other programs.* Washington, DC: NAEYC.

Drotar, D., Baskiewicz, A., Irvin, N., Kennell, J., & Klaus, M. (1975). The adaptation of parents to the birth of an infant with a congenital malformation: A hypothetical model. *Pediatrics, 56*, 710-717.

Dunn, J. (1988a). *Beginnings of social understanding.* Cambridge, MA: Blackwell.

Dunn, J. (1988b). *Normative life events as risk factors in childhood. Studies of psychosocial risk: The power of longitudinal data.* New York: Cambridge University Press.

Dweck, C.S., & Elliot, E.S. (1983). Achievement motivation. In E.M. Hetherington (Ed.) & P.H. Mussen (Series Ed.), *Handbook of child psychology: Vol. 4. Socialization, personality and social development* (pp. 643-691). New York: Wiley.

Eckerman, C.O., Whatley, J.L., & Kutz, S.L. (1975). Growth of social play with peers during the second year of life. *Developmental Psychology, 11*(1), 42-49.

Eder, R.A. (1989). The emergent personologist: The structure and content of 3½, 5½ and 7½-year-olds' concepts of themselves and other persons. *Child Development, 60*(5), 1218-1228.

Eder, R.A., & Mangelsdorf, S.C. (in press). The emotional basis of early personality development: Implications for the emergent self-concept. In S.R. Briggs, R. Hogan, & W.H. Jones (Eds.), *Handbook of personality psychology*. New York: Academic Press.

Elashoff, J., & Snow, R. (1971). *Pygmalion reconsidered*. Worthington, OH: Jones.

Elkind, D. (1981). *The hurried child: Growing up too fast too soon*. Reading, MA: Addison-Wesley.

Elkind, D. (1987). *Miseducation: Preschoolers at risk*. New York: Knopf.

Emde, R. (1983). The pre-representational self and its affective core. *Psychoanalytic Study of the Child, 38*, 165–192.

Emde, R. (1989). Toward a psychoanalytic theory of affect: The organizational model and its propositions. In S.I. Greenspan & G.H. Pollock (Eds.), *The course of life. Vol. I, Infancy* (pp. 165–192). Madison, CT: International Universities Press.

Entwisle, D.R., & Alexander, K.L. (1988). Factors affecting achievement test scores and marks of Black and White first graders. *The Elementary School Journal, 88*(5), 449–471.

Entwisle, D.R., & Hayduk, L.A. (1982). *Early schooling: Cognitive and affective outcomes*. Baltimore, MD: Johns Hopkins University Press.

Epstein, S. (1973). The self-concept revisited as a theory of a theory. *American Psychologist, 28*, 405–416.

Erikson, E. (1950). *Childhood and society* (2nd ed.). New York: Norton.

Featherston, H. (1980). *A difference in the family*. New York: Basic.

Fein, G.G. (1984). The self-building potential of pretend play or "I got a fish, all by myself." In T.D. Yawkey & A.D. Pellegrini (Eds.), *Child's play: Developmental and applied* (pp. 125–142). Hillsdale, NJ: Erlbaum.

Ferguson, C.A. (1977). Baby-talk on a simplified register. In C.E. Snow & C.A. Ferguson (Eds.), *Talking to children: Language input and acquisition*. New York: Cambridge University Press.

Ferris, C. (1980). *A hug just isn't enough*. Washington, DC: Gallaudet College Press.

Field, T.M., Woodson, R., Greenberg, R., & Cohen, D. (1982). Discrimination and imitation of facial expressions by neonates. *Science, 218*, 179–182.

Fischer, K.W., Hand, H.H., Watson, M.W., Van Parys, M.M., & Tucker, J.L. (1984). Putting the child into socialization: The development of social categories in preschool children. In L.G. Katz (Ed.), *Current topics in early childhood education* (pp. 27–72). Norwood, NJ: Ablex.

Fraiberg, S.H. (1959). *The magic years*. New York: Scribner.

Fraiberg, S. (1974). Blind infants and their mothers: An examination of the sign system. In M. Lewis & L. Rosenblum (Eds.), *The effect of the infant on its caregiver* (pp. 215–232). New York: Wiley.

Fraiberg, S. (1975). The development of human attachments in infants blind from birth. *Merrill-Palmer Quarterly, 21*, 315–334.

Fraiberg, S., Adelson, E., & Shapiro, V. (1975). Ghosts in the nursery. *Journal of the American Academy of Child Psychiatry, 14*, 387–421.

Freud, A. (1965). *Normality and pathology in childhood: Assessments of development*. Madison, CT: International Universities Press.

Freud, W.E. (1989a). Notes on some psychological aspects of neonatal intensive care. In S.I. Greenspan & G.H. Pollock (Eds.), *The course of life, Vol. I, Infancy* (pp. 485–501). Madison, CT: International Universities Press.

Freud, W.E. (1989b). Prenatal attachment and bonding. In S. Greenspan & G. Pollock (Eds.), *The course of life, Vol. I, Infancy* (pp. 467–484). Madison, CT: International Universities Press.

Froebel, F. (1987). *The education of man*. New York: Appleton-Century-Crofts.

Gallagher, R.J., Jens, K.G., & O'Donnell, K.J. (1984). The effect of physical status on the affective expression of handicapped infants. *Infant Behavior and Development.*

Gardner, H. (1983). *Frames of mind. The theory of multiple intelligence.* New York: Basic.

Godwin, A., & Schrag, L. (1988). *Setting up for infant care: Guidelines for centers and family day care homes.* Washington, DC: NAEYC.

Goebes, D.D., & Shore, M.E. (1978). Some effects of bicultural and monocultural school environments on personality development. *American Journal of Orthopsychiatry, 48,* 407–498.

Gottman, J., & Parkhurst, J. (1980). A developmental theory of friendship and acquaintanceship processes. In W. Collins (Ed.), *Minnesota Symposium on Child Psychology,* Vol. 13. Hillsdale, NJ: Erlbaum.

Gould, R. (1972). *Child studies through fantasy.* New York: Quadrangle.

Graff, H. (1979). *The social structure in the century city.* New York: Academic.

Greenberg, M.T., & Marvin, R.S. (1979). Attachment patterns in profoundly deaf preschool children. *Merrill-Palmer Quarterly, 25,* 265–279.

Greenberg, P. (1988). Positive self-image. More than just mirrors. *Young Children, 43*(4), 57.

Greenberg, P. (1990). Why not academic preschool? (Part I). *Young Children, 45*(2), 70–80.

Greeno, J.G. (1989). A perspective on thinking. *American Psychologist, 44*(2), 134–141.

Greenspan, S., & Greenspan, N.T. (1985). *First feelings: Milestones in the emotional development of the child.* New York: Viking.

Grossman, K., Grossman, K.E., Spangler, G., Suess, G., & Unzner, L. (1985). Maternal sensitivity and newborns' orientation responses as related to quality of attachment in Northern Germany. In I. Bretherton & E. Waters (Eds.), Growing points in attachment theory and research. *Monographs for the Society for Research in Child Development, 50*(1–2), 233–256.

Haltiwanger, J. (1989). *Behavioral referents of presented self-esteem in young children.* Poster session presented at biennial meeting of the Society for Research in Child Development, Kansas City, Missouri.

Harms, T., & Gifford, R.M. (1980). *Early Childhood Environment Rating Scale.* New York: Teachers College Press.

Harris, P. (1989). *Children and emotion.* Cambridge, MA: Blackwell.

Harrison, A.O., Wilson, M.N., Pine, C.J., Chan, S.Q., & Buriel, R. (1990). Family ecologies of ethnic minority children. *Child Development, 61*(2), 347–362.

Harter, S. (1977). A cognitive-developmental approach to children's expressions of conflicting feelings and a technique to facilitate such expression in play therapy. *Journal of Consulting and Clinical Psychology, 45,* 417–432.

Harter, S. (1983). Developmental perspectives on the self-system. In E.M. Hetherington (Ed.) & P.H. Mussen (Series Ed.), *Handbook of child psychology: Vol. 4. Socialization, personality, and social development* (4th ed.) (pp. 275–386). New York: Wiley.

Harter, S. (1990). Causes, correlates, and the functional role of global self-worth: A life span perspective. In R.J. Sternberg & J. Kolligan (Eds.), *Competence considered* (pp. 67–97). New Haven: Yale University Press.

Harter, S., & Whitesell, N. (1989). Developmental changes in children's emotion concepts. In C. Saarni & P.L. Harris (Eds.), *Children's understanding of emotions* (pp. 81–116). New York: Cambridge University Press.

Hartup, W.W. (1974). Aggression in childhood: Developmental perspectives. *American Psychologist, 19,* 336–341.

Hartup, W.W. (1984). The peer context in middle childhood. In W.A. Collins (Ed.), *Development during middle childhood* (pp. 240–282). Washington, DC: National Academy Press.

Hartup, W., Glazer, J.A., & Charlesworth, R. (1967). Peer reinforcement and sociometric status. *Child Development, 38,* 1017–1024.

Hay, D. (1989, April). *Children's use of defenses and self-esteem management.* Paper presented at the Biennial Meeting of the Society for Research in Child Development, Kansas City, MO.

Hazen, N.L., & Black, B. (1989). Preschool peer communication skills: The role of social status and interaction content. *Child Development, 60*(4), 867–876.

Heath, S.B. (1989). Oral and literate traditions among Black Americans living in poverty. *American Psychologist 44*(2), 367–373.

Heckhausen, H. (1984). Emergent achievement behavior: Some early developments. In J.G. Nicholls (Ed.), *Advances in motivation and achievement: Vol. 3, The development of achievement motivation* (pp. 1–32). Greenwich, CT: JAI Press.

Hetherington, E.M. (1971). Personality development. In L.C. Deighton (Ed.), *The encyclopedia of education,* Vol. 7. New York: Macmillan.

Higgins, E.T., & Parsons, J.E. (1983). Social cognition and the social life of the child: Stages as subcultures. In E.T. Higgins, D.W. Ruble, & W.W. Hartup (Eds.), *Social cognition and social development: A socio-cultural perspective* (pp. 15–62). New York: Cambridge University Press.

Hirsh-Pasek, K., & Cone, J. (1989, April). Hurrying children: How does it affect their academic, creative, and emotional development? In K. Hirsh-Pasek (Chair), *Learning environments in early childhood: Challenge or pressure?* Symposium conducted at the Biennial meeting of the Society for Research in Child Development, Kansas City, MO.

Hitz, R., & Driscoll, A. (1988). Praise or encouragement? New insights into praise: Implications for early childhood teachers. *Young Children, 43*(5), 6–13.

Hoffman, M.L. (1970). Moral development. In P.H. Mussen (Ed.), *Carmichael's manual of child psychology, Vol. 2* (pp. 261–359). New York: Wiley.

Hoffman, M.L. (1984). Interaction of affect and cognition on empathy. In C.E. Izard, J. Kakan, & R.B. Zajonc (Eds.), *Emotions, cognition, and behavior* (pp. 103–131). New York: Cambridge University Press.

Honig, A.S. (1985). Research in review. Compliance, control, and discipline (Parts 1 & 2). *Young Children, 40*(2), 50–58; *40*(3) 47–53.

Honig, A.S. (1987). Research in review. The shy child. *Young Children, 42*(4), 54–64.

Isaacs, S. (1933). *Social development in young children.* London: Routledge & Kegan Paul.

Jacobson, J. (1971). *The determinants of early peer interaction.* Unpublished doctoral dissertation, Harvard University, Cambridge, MA.

Jacobson, J., & Willie, D. (1986). *The influence of attachment pattern on peer interaction at 2 and 3 years.* Paper presented at the International Conference on Infant Studies, New York.

James, W.T. (1890). *The principles of psychology.* New York: Holt.

Jennings, K.D. (1975). Person versus object orientation, social behavior, and intellectual abilities in preschool children. *Developmental Psychology, 11,* 511–519.

Jens, K., & Johnson, N. (1982). Affective development: A window to cognition in young handicapped children. *Topics in Early Childhood Special Education, 2*(2), 17–24.

Jessner, L., Weiger, E., & Foy, J.L. (1970). The development of parental attitudes during pregnancy. In E.J. Anthony & T. Benedek (Eds.), *Parenthood: Its psychology and psychopathology* (pp. 209–244). Boston: Little, Brown.

Kagan, J. (1981). *The second year. The emergence of self-awareness.* Cambridge, MA: Harvard University Press.

Kagan, J., Reznick, J.S., & Gibbons, J. (1989). Inhibited and uninhibited types of children. *Child Development, 60*(4), 838–845.

Kagan, S.L., & Zigler, E.F. (1987). *Early schooling: The national debate.* New Haven: Yale University Press.

Kamii, C. (Ed.). (1990). *Achievement testing in the early grades: The games grown-ups play.* Washington, DC: NAEYC.

Kamii, C., & DeVries, R. (1980). *Group games in early education: Implications of Piaget's theory.* Washington, DC: NAEYC.

Kastein, S., Spaulding, I., & Scharf, B. (1980). *Raising the young blind child: A guide for parents and educators.* New York: Human Sciences Press.

Katz, L.G. (Ed.). (1984). *Current topics in early childhood education, Vol. V.* Norwood, NJ: Ablex.

Katz, L.G. (1985). Dispositions in early childhood education. *ERIC/EECE Bulletin, 18*(2). Urbana, IL: ERIC Clearinghouse on Elementary and Early Childhood Education.

Katz, L.G., & Chard, S.C. (1989). *Engaging children's minds: The project approach.* Norwood, NJ: Ablex.

Kennedy, J.C. (1973). The high-risk maternal-infant acquaintance process. *Nursing Clinics of North America, 8,* 549–556.

King, R. (1978). *All things bright and beautiful?* New York: Wiley.

Klaus, M.H., & Kennell, J.H. (1976). *Maternal-infant bonding.* St. Louis, MO: Mosby.

Klein, M., & Stern, L. (1971). Low birthweight and the battered child syndrome. *American Journal of Disabled Children, 122*(15).

Kohlberg, L. (1976). Moral stages and moralization: Cognitive-developmental approach. In T. Lickona (Ed.), *Moral development and behavior: Theory, research, and social issues* (pp. 31–53). New York: Holt, Rinehart & Winston.

Kohut, H. (1971). *The analysis of the self.* Madison, CT: International Universities Press.

Lamb, M.E. (1977). Father-infant and mother-infant interaction in the first year of life. *Child Development, 48,* 167–181.

Lewis, M., & Brooks-Gunn, J. (1979). *Social cognition and the acquisition of self.* New York: Plenum.

Lewis, M., & Rosenblum, L. (Eds.). (1975). *Friendship and peer relations.* New York: Wiley.

Licht, B.G., & Kistner, J.A. (1986). Motivational problems of learning-disabled children: Individual differences and their implications for treatment. In J.R. Torgesen & B.Y.L. Wong (Eds.), *Psychological and educational perspectives on learning disabilities* (pp. 225–255). Orlando, FL: Academic.

Londerville, S., & Main, M. (1981). Security of attachment, compliance, and maternal training methods in the second year of life. *Developmental Psychology, 17,* 289–299.

Maccoby, E.E., & Jacklin, C. (1974). *The psychology of sex differences.* Stanford, CA: Stanford University Press.

Maccoby, E.E., & Martin, J.A. (1983). Socialization in the context of the family: Parent-child interaction. In E.M. Hetherington (Ed.) & P.H. Mussen (Series Ed.), *Handbook of child psychology: Vol. 4. Socialization, personality, and social development* (pp. 1–102). New York: Wiley.

Mack, J.E. (1985). Self-esteem and its development. In J.E. Mack & S.L. Ablon

(Eds.), *The development and sustenance of self-esteem in childhood* (pp. 1–41). Madison, CT: International Universities Press.

Mahler, M.S., Pine, F., & Bergman, A. (1975). *The psychological birth of the human infant.* New York: Basic.

Main, M. (1973). *Play, exploration, and competence as related to child-adult attachment.* Unpublished doctoral dissertation, Johns Hopkins University, Baltimore, MD.

Main, M. (1985). *An adult attachment classification system.* Paper presented at the biennial meeting of the Society for Research in Child Development, Toronto.

Main, M., Kaplan, N., & Cassidy, J. (1985). Security in infancy, childhood, and adulthood: A move to the level of representation. In I. Bretherton & E. Waters (Eds.), Growing points of attachment theory and research (pp. 66–106). *Monographs of the Society for Research in Child Development 50*(1–2).

Markus, H., Cross, S., & Wurf, E. (1990). The role of the self-system in competence. In R.J. Sternberg & J. Kolligan, (Eds.), *Competence considered* (pp. 205–225). New Haven: Yale University Press.

Markus, H., & Wurf, E. (1987). The dynamic self-concept: A social psychological perspective. In M.R. Rosenzweig & L.W. Porter (Eds.), *Annual review of psychology, 38,* 299–338.

Marshall, N.R., Hogrenes, J.R., & Goldstein, S. (1973). Verbal interactions: Mothers and their retarded children vs. mothers and their nonretarded children. *American Journal of Mental Deficiency, 77,* 415–417.

Martens, R., Christina, R.W., Harvey, J.S., Jr., & Sharkey, B.J. (1981). *Coaching young athletes.* Champaign, IL: Human Kinetics Publishers.

Matas, L., Arend, R., & Sroufe, L.A. (1978). Continuity of adaptation in the second year: The relationship between quality of attachment and later competence. *Child Development, (49)*3, 547–556.

McCall, R.B., Eichhorn, D., & Hogarty, P. (1977). Transitions in early mental development. *Monographs of the Society for Research in Child Development, 42,* (3, Serial No. 171).

McCubbin, H.I., Nevin, R.S., Larsen, A., Comeau, J., Patterson, J., Cauble, A.E., & Striker, K. (1981). *Families coping with cerebral palsy.* St. Paul: University of Minnesota, Family Social Science.

Mecca, A.M. (1989). Foreword. In A.M. Mecca, N.J. Smelser, & J. Vasconellos (Eds.), *The social importance of self-esteem* (pp. vii–ix). Berkeley, CA: University of California Press.

Mecca, A.M., Smelser, N.J., & Vasconellos, J. (1989). *The social importance of self-esteem.* Berkeley, CA: University of California Press.

Meltzoff, A.N., & Moore, M.K. (1977). Imitation of facial and manual gestures by human neonates. *Science, 198,* 75–78.

Milner, D. (1983). *Children and race* (2nd ed.). Harmondsworth: Penguin.

Mintzer, D., Als, H., Tronick, E.Z., & Brazelton, T.B. (1984). Parenting an infant with a birth defect: The regulation of self-esteem. *Psychoanalytic Study of the Child, 39,* 561–589.

Miyake, K., Chen, S., & Campos, J.J. (1985). Infant temperament, mother's mode of interaction, and attachment in Japan: An interim report. In I. Bretherton & E. Waters (Eds.), Growing points in attachment theory and research (pp. 276–297). *Monographs of the Society for Research in Child Development, 50*(1–2).

Montessori, M. (1973). *The Montessori method.* Cambridge, MA: Bentley.

Moore, G.T. (1980). The application of research to the design of therapeutic play environments for exceptional children. In W. Cruikshank (Ed.), *Approaches to learning* (pp. 201–229). Syracuse, NY: Syracuse University Press.

Moore, G.T. (1985). State of the art in play environments. In J.L. Frost & S.

Sunderlin (Eds.), *When children play* (pp. 171–192). Wheaton, MD: Association for Childhood Education International.

Moore, G.T. (1986). Effects of the spatial definition of behavioral settings on children's behavior: A quasi-experimental field study. *Journal of Environmental Psychology, 6,* 205–231.

Moore, G.T. (1987). The physical environment and cognitive development in child-care centers. In C.S. Weinstein & T.G. David (Eds.), *Spaces for children: The built environment and child development* (pp. 41–67). New York: Plenum.

Moore, G.T., Cohen, U., & McGinty, T. (1979). *Planning and design guidelines: Childcare centers and outdoor play environments.* Milwaukee: University of Wisconsin, Milwaukee Center for Architecture and Urban Planning Research.

Mordock, J.B. (1979). The separation-individuation process and developmental disabilities. *Exceptional Children, 46,* 176–184.

Mueller, E., & Vandell, D. (1979). Infant-interaction. In J.D. Osofsky (Ed.), *Handbook of infant development* (pp. 591–622). New York: Wiley.

Murphy, L.B., Mintzer, D., & Lipsett, L.P. (1989). Psychoanalytic views of infancy. In S.I. Greenspan & G.H. Pollock (Eds.), *The course of life, Vol. I, Infancy* (pp. 561–642). Madison, CT: International Universities Press.

Musick, J.S., & Householder, J. (1986). *Infant development: From theory to practice.* Belmont, CA: Wadsworth.

Nachman, P., & Stern, D.N. (1983). *Recall memory for emotional experience in prelinguistic infants.* Paper presented at the National Clinical Infancy Fellows Conference, Yale University, New Haven, CT.

Nelson, J. (1987). *Positive discipline.* New York: Ballantine.

Nelson, K.E., & Gruendel, J. (1979). At morning it's lunchtime: A scripted view of children's dialogues. *Discourse Processes, 2,* 73–94.

Nicholls, J.G. (1990). What is ability and why are we mindful of it? A developmental perspective. In R.J. Sternberg & J. Kolligian (Eds.), *Competence considered* (pp. 11–40). New Haven: Yale University Press.

Olds, A.R. (1979). Designing developmentally optimal classrooms for children with special needs. In S. Meisels (Ed.), *Special education and developmental perspectives of young children with special needs* (pp. 91–138). Baltimore, MD: University Park Press.

Olweus P. (1978). *Aggression in the schools.* Washington: Hemisphere.

Paley, V.G. (1984). *Boys and girls: Superheroes in the doll corner.* Chicago: University of Chicago Press.

Paley, V.G. (1986). *Mollie is 3: Growing up in school.* Chicago: University of Chicago Press.

Paley, V.G. (1988). *Bad guys don't have birthdays: Fantasy play at 4.* Chicago: University of Chicago Press.

Papoušek, M., & Papoušek, H. (1979). Early ontogeny of human social interaction: Its biological roots and social dimensions. In M. Von Cranach, K. Foppa, W. Lepenies, & P. Ploog (Eds.), *Human ethology: Claims and limits of a new discipline* (pp. 456–478). New York: Cambridge University Press.

Passer, M.W. (1988). Psychological issues in determining children's age-readiness for competition. In F.L. Smoll, R.A. Magill, & M.J. Ash (Eds.), *Children in sports* (pp. 67–78). Champaign, IL: Human Kinetics Books.

Patterson, J.G., DeBarsyshe, B.D., & Ramsey, E. (1989). A developmental perspective on antisocial behavior. *American Psychologist, 44*(2), 329–335.

Peck, J.T., McCaig, G., & Sapp, M.E. (1988). *Kindergarten policies: What is best for children?* (NAEYC Research Monograph, Vol. 2). Washington, DC: NAEYC.

Phillips, D.A., & Zimmerman, M. (1990). The developmental course of perceived competence and incompetence among competent children. In R.J. Sternberg &

J. Korligan, Jr. (Eds.), *Competence considered* (pp. 41–66). New Haven: Yale University Press.

Piaget, J. (1952). *The origins of intelligence in children.* Madison, CT: International Universities Press.

Piaget, J. (1954). *The construction of reality in the child.* (M. Cook, Trans.). New York: Basic.

Pitcher, E.G., & Schultz, L.H. (1984). *Boys and girls at play — The development of sex roles.* New York: Praeger.

Power, T.G., & Parke, R.D. (1983). Patterns of mother and father play with their 8-month-old infant: A multiple analysis approach. *Infant Behavior, 6,* 453–459.

Prechtl, H.F.R. (1963). The mother-child interaction in babies with minimal brain damage. In B.M. Foss (Ed.), *Determinants of infant behavior, Vol. 2.* New York: Wiley.

Prechtl, H.F.R., & Beintema, O. (1984). *The neurological examination of the full-term newborn infant.* London: Heinemann.

Prescott, E. (1987). The environment as organizer of intent in child-care settings. In T.G. David & C.S. Weinstein (Eds.), *Spaces for children: The built environment and child development* (pp. 73–88). New York: Plenum.

Prescott, E., & David, T.G. (1976). The effects of the physical environment on day care. Concept paper prepared for the U.S. Department of Health, Education and Welfare, Office of Child Development.

Prescott, E., & Jones, E. (1967). *Group day care as a child-rearing environment.* Pasadena, CA: Pacific Oaks College.

Provence, S., & Lipton, R.C. (1962). *Infants in institutions.* Madison, CT: International Universities Press.

Putallaz, M., & Gottman, J.M. (1981). An interactional model of children's entry into peer groups. *Child Development, 52,* 986–994.

Renick, M.J., & Harter, S. (1989). Impact of social comparisons on the developing self-perceptions of learning disabled students. *Journal of Educational Psychology, 81,* 631–638.

Resch, R. (1979). Hatching in the human infant at the beginning of separation-individuation: What it is and what it looks like. *Psychoanalytic Study of the Child, 34,* 421–444.

Resnick, L.B. (1989). Developing mathematical knowledge. *American Psychologist, 44*(2), 162–169.

Rogoff, B., & Wertsch, J.V. (Eds.). (1984). Children's learning in the "zone of proximal development." *New Directions for Child Development, 23,* San Francisco: Jossey-Bass.

Rosen, J.L. (1968). Personality and first-year teacher's relationships with children. *School Review, 76,* 294–311.

Rosen, J.L. (1972). Matching teachers with children. *School Review, 80,* 409–431.

Rosen, J.L. (1975). Perceptions of the childhood self and teacher-child relations. (ERIC Document Reproduction Service No. ED 115 609)

Rosenberg, M. (1979). *Conceiving the self.* New York: Basic.

Rosenthal, R., & Jacobson, L. (1968). *Pygmalion in the classroom: Teacher expectation and pupils' intellectual development.* New York: Holt, Rinehart & Winston.

Roskies, E. (1972). *Abnormality and normality: The mothering of thalidomide children.* Ithaca, NY: Cornell University.

Rothbaum, F., & Weisz, J.R. (1989). *Child psychopathology and the quest for control.* Newburg Park, CA: Sage.

Rubin, K.N., Fein, G.G., & Vandenberg, B. (1983). Play. In E.M. Hetherington (Ed.) & P.H. Mussen (Series Ed.), *Handbook of child psychology: Vol. 4. Socialization, personality, and social development* (pp. 698–774). New York: Wiley.

Rubin, Z. (1980). *Children's friendships.* Cambridge: Harvard University Press.

Rutter, M. (1987). Psychosocial resilience and protective mechanisms. *American Journal of Orthopsychiatry, 57*(3), 316–331.

Sander, L.W. (1975). Infant and caretaking environment. In E.J. Anthony (Ed.), *Explorations in child psychiatry* (pp. 129–166). New York: Plenum.

Schachter, F.F. (1979). *Everyday mother talk to toddlers: Early intervention.* New York: Academic.

Schachter, F.F., & Strage, A.A. (1982). Adults' talk and children's language development. In S.G. Moore & C.R. Cooper (Eds.), *The young child: Reviews of research, Vol. 3* (pp. 79–96). Washington, DC: NAEYC.

Scheirer, M.A., & Krout, R.E. (1979). Increasing educational achievement via self-concept changes. *Review of Educational Research, 49,* 131–150.

Schirrmacher, R. (1986). Talking with young children about their art. *Young Children, 41*(5), 3–10.

Schlesinger, H.S., & Meadow, K.P. (1972). *Sound and sign: Childhood deafness and mental health.* Berkeley, CA: University of California Press.

Schofield, J.N. (1981). Complementary and conflicting identities: Images and interactions in an interracial school. In S.R. Asher & J.M. Gottman (Eds.), *The development of children's friendships* (pp. 53–90). New York: Cambridge University Press.

Schwartzman, H. (1978). *Transformations: The anthropology of children's play.* New York: Plenum.

Scott, E.P., Jan, J.E., & Freeman, R.D. (1977). *Can't your child see?* Baltimore, MD: University Park Press.

Selman, R., & Jaquette, D. (1977). Stability and oscillation in interpersonal awareness: A clinical-developmental analysis. In C.B. Keasey (Ed.), *Nebraska symposium in motivation* (pp 261–304). Lincoln, NE: University of Nebraska Press.

Serbin, L.A., Tronick, I.J., & Sternglanz, S.H. (1977). Shaping cooperative cross-sex play. *Child Development, 48*(3), 924–929.

Shepard, L.A., & Smith, M.E. (1986). Synthesis of research on school readiness and kindergarten retention. *Educational Leadership, 44,* 78–86.

Shotwell, J.M., Wolf, D., & Gardner, H. (1979). Exploring early symbolization: Styles in achievement. In B. Sutton-Smith (Ed.), *Play and learning* (pp. 127–156). New York: Gardner.

Shure, M.B., & Spivack, G. (1978). *Problem-solving techniques in childrearing.* San Francisco: Jossey-Bass.

Siegel, M., & Storey, R.M. (1985). Daycare and children's conceptions of moral and social rules. *Child Development, 56,* 1001–1008.

Sizemore, B.A. (1987). The effective African-American elementary school. In G.W. Noblit & W.T. Pink (Eds.), *School in social context: Qualitative studies* (pp. 175–202). Norwood, NJ: Ablex.

Slade, A. (1986). Symbolic play and separation-individuation: A naturalistic study. *Bulletin of the Menninger Clinic, 50,* 541–563.

Slukin, A.M., & Smith, P.K. (1977). Two approaches to the concept of dominance in preschool children. *Child Development, 48,* 917–923.

Smetana, J.G. (1981). Preschool children's conception of moral and social rules. *Child Development, 52,* 1333–1336.

Smetana, J.G. (1984). Toddlers' social interactions regarding moral and conventional transgressions. *Child Development, 55,* 1767–1776.

Smetana, J.G. (1985). Preschool children's conceptions of transgressions: Effects of varying moral and conventional domain-related attributes. *Developmental Psychology, 21,* 18–29.

Smetana, J.G., Kelly, M., & Twentyman, C.T. (1984). Abused, neglected and non-maltreated children's conceptions of moral and socio-conventional transgressions. *Child Development, 55,* 277–287.

Smith, P.K., & Daglish, L. (1977). Sex differences in infant and parent behavior. *Child Development, 48,* 1250–1254.

Solnit, A., & Stark, M.H. (1961). Mourning and the birth of a defective child. *Psychoanalytic Study of the Child, 16,* 523–537.

Sorce, J.F., Emde, R.N., Campos, J.J., & Kinnert, M.D. (1985). Maternal emotional signaling: Its effects on the visual cliff behavior of 1-year-olds. *Developmental Psychology, 21,* 195–200.

Spitz, R. (1946). Anaclitic depression. *Psychoanalytic Study of the Child, 2,* 313–342.

Spitz, R. (1965). *The first year of life: A psychoanalytic study of normal and deviant development of object relations.* Madison, CT: International Universities Press.

Sroufe, L.A. (1983). Infant-caregiver attachment and patterns of adaptation in preschool: The roots of maladaption and competence. In M. Perlmutter (Ed.), *Minnesota Symposium in Child Psychology, 16,* 41–81.

Stern, D. (1985). *The interpersonal world of the infant.* New York: Basic.

Stern, D. (1989, August). *The world of infant research and adult psychotherapy.* Cape Cod Symposium, Cape Cod, MA.

Stern, D.N. (1974). Mother and infant at play: The dyadic interaction involving facial, vocal and gaze behaviors. In M. Lewis & L.A. Rosenblum (Eds.), *The effect of the infant on its caregiver* (pp. 187–213). New York: Wiley.

Sternberg, R.J., & Kolligan, J. (Eds.). (1990). *Competence considered.* New Haven: Yale University Press.

Stevenson, H.W., Chen, C., & Uttal, D.H. (1990). Beliefs and achievement: A study of Black, White, and Hispanic children. *Child Development, 61,* 508–523.

Stevenson, H.W., & Lee, S. (1990). Contexts of achievement. *Monographs of the Society for Research in Child Development, 55* (1–2).

Stipek, D., & Daniels, D. (1988). Declining perceptions of competence: A consequence of changes in the child or the educational environment? *Journal of Educational Psychology, 80,* 352–356.

Stipek, D., & Mac Iver, D. (1989). Developmental change in children's assessment of intellectual competence. *Child Development, 60,* 521–538.

Stone, N.W., & Chesney, B.H. (1978). Attachment behaviors in handicapped infants. *Mental Retardation, 16,* 8–12.

Strauss, M.S. (1979). Abstraction of prototypical information by adults and 10-month-old infants. *Journal of Experimental Psychology: Human Learning and Memory, 5,* 618–632.

Strayer, J. (1983). *Emotional and cognitive components of children's empathy.* Paper presented at the meeting of the Society for Research in Child Development, Toronto.

Strein, N. (1988). Classroom-based elementary school affective education programs: A critical review. *Psychology in the Schools, 25,* 288–296.

Sugarman, L. (1986). *Life-span development: Concepts, theories, and interventions.* London: Methuen.

Sullivan, H.S. (1953). *The interpersonal theory of psychiatry.* New York: Norton.

Sutton-Smith, B., & Kelly-Byrne, D. (1984). The idealization of play. In P.K. Smith (Ed.), *Play in animals and humans* (pp. 305–320). London: Blackwell.

Tharp, R.G. (1989). Psychocultural variables and constants: Effects on teaching and learning in schools. *American Psychologist, 44*(2), 349–359.

Thomas, A., & Chess, S. (1977). *Temperament and development.* New York: Brunner/Mazel.

Tobin, J.J., Wu, D.Y.H., & Davidson, D.H. (1989). *Preschool in three cultures: Japan, China, and the United States.* New Haven: Yale University Press.

Tolpin, M. (1971). On the beginning of a cohesive self. *Psychoanalytic Study of the Child, 26,* 316–352.

Tronick, E.Z. (1989). Emotions and emotional communication in infants. *American Psychologist, 44*(2), 112–119.

Tronick, E.Z., Cohn, J., & Shea, E. (1984). The transfer of affect between mothers and infants. In T.B. Brazelton & M.M. Yogman (Eds.), *Affective development in infancy* (pp. 11–25). Norwood, NJ: Ablex.

Vaughn, B., Kopp, C.B., & Krakow, J.B. (1984). The emergence and consolidation of self-control from 18 to 30 months of age: Normative trends and individual differences. *Child Development, 55,* 990–1004.

Vondra, J., Barnett, D., & Cicchetti, D. (1989). Perceived and actual competence among maltreated and comparison school children. *Development and Psychopathology, 1,* 237–255.

Vygotsky, L.S. (1978). *Mind and society: The development of higher psychological processes.* Cambridge: Harvard University Press.

Washington, V. (1982). Racial differences in teacher perceptions of first and fourth grade pupils on selected characteristics. *Journal of Negro Education, 51,* 60–72.

Watson, J.S., & Ramey, C.T. (1972). Reactions to response-contingent stimulation in early infancy. *Merrill-Palmer Quarterly, 18,* 219–227.

Wedell-Monnig, J., & Lumley, J.M. (1980). Child deafness and mother-child interaction. *Child Development, 51,* 766–774.

Weinraub, M., & Frankel, J. (1977). Sex differences in parent-infant interaction during freeplay, departure and separation. *Child Development, 48,* 1240–1249.

Weissbourd, B., & Musick, J. (Eds.). (1981). *Infants: Their social environment.* Washington, DC: NAEYC.

Weisz, J.R., Bromfeld, R., Vines, D.L., & Weiss, B. (1985). Cognitive development, helpless behavior and labeling effects in the lives of the mentally retarded. In F.J. Morrison, C. Lord, & D.P. Keating (Eds.), *Applied developmental psychology* (pp. 147–168). New York: Academic.

White, B.L. (1985). *The first 3 years of life* (rev. ed.). Englewood Cliffs, NJ: Prentice-Hall.

White, B.L. (1988). *Educating the infant and toddler.* Lexington, MA: Lexington Books.

White, R.W. (1963). Ego and reality in psychoanalytic theory. *Psychological Issues, Monograph 3.*

Winnicott, D.W. (1965). *The maturational processes and the facilitating environment.* Madison, CT: International Universities Press.

Wolf, D., & Gardner, H. (1978). Style and sequence in early symbolic play. In M. Franklin & N. Smith (Eds.), *New directions in child development: Early symbolization Vol. 3.* (pp. 117–138). Hillsdale, NJ: Erlbaum.

Wolff, P.H. (1966). The causes, control and organization of behavior in the neonate. *Psychological Issues, 5* (17).

Wood, D.J., Bruner, J.S., & Ross, G. (1976). The role of tutoring in problem solving. *Journal of Child Psychology and Psychiatry, 17*(2), 89–100.

Wood, D., McMahon, L., & Cranstoun, Y. (1980). *Working with under fives.* Ypsilanti, MI: High/Scope.

Woodcock, L. (1941). *Life and ways of the 2-year-old.* New York: Basic.

Wylie, R. (1974). *The self-concept: A review of methological considerations and measuring instruments, Vol 1* (rev. ed.). Lincoln, NE: University of Nebraska Press.

Wylie, R. (1979). *The self-concept, Vol. 2. Theory and research and selected topics.* Lincoln, NE: University of Nebraska Press.

Zigler, E., & Long, M. (1986). The "gourmet baby" and the "little wild flower." *Bulletin of the National Center for Clinical Infant Programs, 7*(2), 8–12.

Other related books by NAEYC

Bredekamp, S. (Ed.). (1987). *Developmentally appropriate practice in early childhood programs serving children from birth through age 8.* Washington, DC: National Association for the Education of Young Children.

Greenberg, P. (1991). *Character development: Encouraging self-esteem & self-discipline in infants, toddlers, & two-year-olds.* Washington, DC: National Association for the Education of Young Children.

McCracken, J.B. (Ed.). (1986). *Reducing stress in young children's lives.* Washington, DC: National Association for the Education of Young Children.

Other books in NAEYC's monograph series

Peck, J.T., McCaig, G., & Sapp, M.E. (1988). *Kindergarten policies: What is best for children?* Washington, DC: National Association for the Education of Young Children.

Phillips, D.A. (Ed.). (1987). *Quality in child care: What does research tell us?* Washington, DC: National Association for the Education of Young Children.

Powell, D.R. (1989). *Families and early childhood programs.* Washington, DC: National Association for the Education of Young Children.

Information about NAEYC

NAEYC is . . .

. . . a membership-supported organization of people committed to fostering the growth and development of children from birth through age eight. Membership is open to all who share a desire to serve and act on behalf of the needs and rights of young children.

NAEYC provides . . .

. . . educational services and resources to adults who work with and for children, including

- *Young Children,* *the* journal for early childhood educators
- **Books, posters, brochures, and videos** to expand your knowledge and commitment to young children, with topics including infants, curriculum, research, discipline, teacher education, and parent involvement
- An **Annual Conference** that brings people from all over the country to share their expertise and advocate on behalf of children and families
- **Week of Young Child** celebrations sponsored by NAEYC Affiliate Groups across the nation to call public attention to the needs and rights of children and families
- **Insurance plans** for individuals and programs
- **Public affairs information** for knowledgeable advocacy efforts at all levels of government and through the media
- The **National Academy of Early Childhood Programs,** a voluntary accreditation system for high-quality programs for children
- The **National Institute for Early Childhood Professional Development,** providing resources and services to improve professional preparation and development of early childhood educators
- The **Information Service,** a centralized source of information sharing, distribution, and collaboration

For free information about membership, publications, or other NAEYC services . . .

. . . call NAEYC at 202–232–8777 or 800–424–2460, or write to the National Association for the Education of Young Children, 1834 Connecticut Avenue, N.W., Washington, DC 20009–5786.